30 DAYS

TO

A NEW YOU

CHANGED

GLENN M. HAMEL

Changed

© Glenn Hamel

All rights reserved. No part of this publication may be reproduced, stored or transmitted in any form or by any means, electronic, mechanical, photocopying, recording, scanning, or otherwise without written permission from the publisher. It is illegal to copy this book, post it to a website, or distribute it by any other means without permission.

Unless otherwise noted, Scripture is taken from the King James Version. Scripture quotations marked NKJV are from the New King James Version of the Bible. © (1982), Thomas Nelson, Inc. Scripture quotations marked (NIV) are taken from the Holy Bible New International Version® (NIV®), © 1973, 1978, 1984 by International Bible Society. Used by permission of Zondervan. All rights reserved. Scripture quotations marked NLT are from the New Living Translation. © 1996, 2004, 2007, 2013, Tyndale House Foundation. New American Standard NEW AMERICAN STANDARD Bible © 1960, 1962, 1963, 1968, 1971, 1972, 1973, 1975, 1977,1995 by THE LOCKMAN FOUNDATION

Changed, 90 Days To A New You
Copyright © 2023 Glenn Hamel
ISBN: 979-8-9861244-4-5
Lighthouse Publishing

Pastor Glenn

Changed

Week 1 — **10**

 Needing A Change — *12*
 The Plight — *14*
 Self-Made — *16*
 My Way — *18*
 Planting — *20*
 Family Traits — *22*
 Deserving Death — *24*

Week 2 — **26**

 God Can Do It — *28*
 Touching Jesus — *30*
 Change of Heart — *32*
 Free — *34*
 Something New — *36*
 God Guides — *38*
 Broken Chains — *40*

Week 3 — **42**

 Believe or Believe — *44*
 Children of God — *46*
 Forgiven & Forgotten — *48*
 Healed & Changed — *50*
 Living It Up — *52*
 Under Attack — *54*
 Sealed & Delivered — *56*

Week 4 — **58**

 Bitterness — *60*
 Check Yourself — *62*
 Deep Inside — *64*

Comparing	*66*
Disqualified	*68*
Fall Short	*70*
Did You Say Obey	*72*

Week 5 — **74**

Confession	*76*
Guilty	*78*
I'm Sorry	*80*
Power in Prayer	*82*
Disclosed	*84*
Truth	*86*
Purified	*88*

Week 6 — **90**

In His Image	*92*
On My Side	*94*
All Things	*96*
My Choice	*98*
Pressing On	*100*
Undivided	*102*
No Yoking	*104*

Week 7 — **106**

He Cares	*108*
Shape Me	*110*
Good Name	*112*
Chosen	*114*
New Name	*116*
God-itude	*118*
Whose Plan	*120*

Changed

Week 8 — 122
- *Handiwork* — 124
- *Called Out* — 126
- *Begrudged* — 128
- *Friend of God* — 130
- *Child of God* — 132
- *Majestic* — 134
- *Giving Back* — 136

Week 9 — 138
- *Complete* — 140
- *Worship* — 142
- *Whose Battle Is It* — 144
- *Selflessness* — 146
- *Love* — 148
- *Squeezed* — 150
- *Don't Give Up* — 152

Week 10 — 154
- *Worthy* — 156
- *Overcomer* — 158
- *Strive* — 160
- *Hang On* — 162
- *He Did It* — 164
- *Pure* — 166
- *Holy* — 168

Week 11 — 170
- *First Place* — 172
- *Loving Others* — 174
- *Debt-Free* — 176

  Humility   *178*

  First & Second   *180*

  Called   *182*

  Rule   *184*

Week 12   **186**

  Helping Hands   *188*

  Eternal Life   *190*

  Eternity   *192*

  Displayed   *194*

  Mansion   *196*

  Separated   *198*

  Lukewarm   *200*

Week 13   **202**

  True Love   *204*

  Gift of God   *206*

  Power   *208*

  Fruit   *210*

  Grace   *212*

  Raised to Life   *214*

Wrap Up   **216**

  Spirit, Not Flesh   *216*

  About the Author   *219*

Changed

Week 1

> *"Our best thinking and best efforts have gotten us where we are today."*

Have you been struggling? Has your life been in turmoil? Have you found it challenging to make lasting, positive changes in your life? Have you been stuck in the dos and don'ts of religion? Have you tried everything only to fall back into your same old habits and behaviors? If you're tired of doing the same thing over and over again, expecting different results, then I encourage you to set aside some time for the next 90 days and allow God to transform you day by day.

Changed, 90 Days To A New You is designed to break the bondage of sin, the chains of religion, and the negative thought patterns that have destroyed you and held you back. The goal is to help you can find a life-changing deep, personal relationship with the Lord that will mold and shape you into who He created you to be. There's an old saying, "You only get what you give." The same is true on your journey to a "New You." This devotional's impact on your life remains dependent on how sincerely you engage with it and how open you are for God to work within you. If you are hungry for a life of impact, purpose, and peace, if you are desperate for God to transform you, then the next 90 days will be profound.

The fact you are reading this already suggests you are aware of areas in your life which need adjusting and you know only God can truly complete the work necessary in your life. Let me assure you that the Scriptural truths within this devotional will not come back void. If you apply these truths and let God have His way in your life, you will be who He created you to be. You will be free, you will be victorious, and you will have the abundant life He has promised you.

Unfortunately, many who embark on this journey will fail to apply the Word to their lives and will not diligently work through the exercises. The majority will make a great start and even begin to apply the Word to their lives, but they will not complete it. Half-hearted and sporadic application of His Word and the teachings in this devotional will fail to bring about significant change. An uncommitted effort will cause those who refuse to take responsibility for their behaviors to lay the blame on everyone but themselves. Because of these tendencies, I remind you that shallow and insincere surrender will not yield lasting results.

The Good News is, a select few will thoroughly read this devotional, engage with the lessons, and discover true transformation through a life surrendered to Christ. The truth is, God has paved the way for your victory. His completed work has already provided a path to freedom, and He desires a relationship with you. "A New You" is about establishing a correct relationship with the Lord, which will satisfy the empty spaces in your life and bring forth the abundant life that Jesus has promised each of us.

Changed

Now, let's address the obvious—change is difficult and often even seems impossible. If changing your life for the better was as simple as just talking about it, then we would have already made the necessary changes and wouldn't need a devotional to help us. As addressed in my book "Created: Designed by God," you will see how our personalities, character traits, strengths, and weaknesses seem unchangeable, as if they are chiseled in stone. These traits begin in our mother's womb and result from a combination of parental DNA, maternal stress, in utero trauma, maternal trauma, environmental influences, and spiritual laws.

The worst part of trying to change our character is that many of the factors that have shaped us have nothing to do with our decisions or actions. Change becomes even more complicated and seemingly impossible when we consider the spiritual laws that affect us—generational curses, bitterness, unforgiveness, soul ties, negative expectations, and the laws of sowing and reaping, including multiplication and delay. Considering the number of factors that dictate who we are which are entirely out of our control, you may wonder why we even seek to change or work through this devotional. Matthew 19:26 states, "Jesus looked at them and said, 'With man this is impossible, but with God all things are possible.'" Jesus Himself proclaimed that with God, all things are possible. This means that real, lasting change is not only possible but is promised through God. A complete transformation is explained within 2 Corinthians 5:17; "Therefore, if anyone is in Christ, the new creation has come: The old has gone, the new is here!"

By firmly trusting that God's promises will come to pass, we can confidently seek to allow Him to change who we are and transform us into the identity He has designed for us. We no longer need to repeat the same old things, hoping it will be different this time. Instead, we can be renewed and transformed by the power of God.

Before we embark on the process of allowing God to change us, there is one last point we must address. We will not attempt to make these changes solely within our own abilities. Merely striving and doing things differently may create the illusion of successful change in our lives, but unfortunately, it will not last, and it won't bring significant transformation. As I shared in my book "*Created*," the only change we can achieve within ourselves is to be more or less of something. However, the underlying problem remains—we are still the same at our core, grappling with our deeply ingrained identities. We are not seeking a temporary improvement of character or a mere religious facade through this devotional. Instead, we desire to help you prepare your heart and mind so that you can allow God to reshape, redesign, and reconcile you to Himself.

The "New You" will reflect the person God created you to be. This "New You" will live purposefully, aligning with God's original design for you and humanity. The "New You" will not be defined by life's circumstances but will walk in God's authority, fulfilling His purposes on earth.

If you are ready to make lasting change, discover the "New You," understand your purpose, and fulfill it, I invite you to pray with me.

"Father, in Jesus' name, I ask you to prepare my heart and mind to receive what you want to say. Remove any preconceived ideas and understandings that may hinder Your work, and help me be open to Your guidance. I thank You for paying the penalty of my sin and saving me. As Your chosen, I surrender my life to You and declare that You are my Lord and Savior. Amen."

DAY 1
NEEDING A CHANGE

> *Romans 7:18-19*
>
> *"18 And I know that nothing good lives in me, that is, in my sinful nature. I want to do what is right, but I can't. 19 I want to do what is good, but I don't. I don't want to do what is wrong, but I do it anyway."*

Our passage of Scripture today describes the conundrum that all of us live in: We do not do what we want to do, and we end up doing what we don't want to do. If you have read my book "*Created, Designed By God,*" you probably already understand why we are who we are, how our personalities are formed in utero, and that many of the driving forces behind our actions are not even caused by our own making. Knowing where our behaviors stem from and why we are drawn to them helps explain the struggle of not doing what we want and doing what we don't want.

I don't need to explain this, but for many of us, our lives are an absolute mess and need significant change. Regardless of your background, the significance of your needs, or even your personal experiences, the first step must be taken before we can dream of finding the abundant life that Christ has promised us.

For those familiar with the 12 step program, you should already know the First Step is to admit we are powerless over our addictions and dysfunctional behaviors and that our lives are unmanageable. Throughout this devotional, we will be applying and using the 12 steps. These steps are vital in helping us know how to surrender to God and allow Him to make the necessary changes we need. You do not have to be an addict to apply these steps to your life. However, all of us, whether we have addictive personalities or simply struggle to serve the Lord faithfully, should have no problem admitting we need God's help to transform our lives. If you struggle with addiction, I want to encourage you that although this devotion is not specifically geared towards overcoming substance abuse, the lessons within are just as applicable.

Our passage today identifies Paul's inability and our own inability to make any lasting change apart from Christ. Being born into sin, having our very formation in the womb affected by sin, and being impacted by those generational curses passed down to us by our forefathers is why we have failed to find the change we so desperately need. Understanding all of this may make you feel hopeless, as if you can do nothing to improve your life and find the peace you desire.

Coming to the end of our ability is very good as this is how we can take the First Step, which is admitting that we are powerless and recognizing we are incapable of delivering ourselves and changing the direction of our life. In today's reflections, we want to identify the driving forces behind our personalities and behaviors. Understanding why we do what we do will only help us solidify our need for God to intervene. Causing us to recognize that many of the life-crippling character traits we fight against are not even our fault will hopefully allow us to forgive ourselves. This forgiveness, in turn, will free us to run to the One who can and will change the very makeup of who we are.

Changed

Day 1 Exercises

1. Objectively describe your life and what your best efforts have failed to achieve.

_____
_____
_____
_____
_____
_____
_____
_____

2. In what areas of your life are you satisfied?

_____
_____
_____
_____
_____
_____
_____
_____

3. Do you feel God is satisfied with the areas in which you are satisfied?

_____
_____
_____
_____
_____
_____
_____
_____

4. List specific behaviors that seem to control your actions.

_____
_____
_____
_____
_____
_____
_____
_____

DAY 2
THE PLIGHT

> *Romans 8:7*
>
> *"The mind governed by the flesh is hostile to God; it does not submit to God's law, nor can it do so."*

In our passage today, the term "governed" is used to describe how the flesh rules over the mind, controlling our actions and our behaviors. According to the Merriam-Webster dictionary, "governed" means to control and direct with continuous sovereign authority. In simple terms, our fleshly nature controls our thinking, making it impossible for us to change our behaviors and actions on our own.

It is important to understand that the concept of flesh goes beyond our physical bodies, which will eventually cease to function. In the Bible, the flesh is defined as our sinful nature, characterized by our lust and our desires (1 John 2:16). Living in the "flesh state," we are hostile to God and His law, the Bible. Many of us can relate to this condition, as we have experienced moments when our sinful nature has controlled us, leading us to reject, deny, and even mock others for their beliefs. The latter part of today's passage confirms our ongoing struggle to change, stating that we cannot submit to God or His law when controlled and governed by the flesh.

Before accepting Christ as our Lord and Savior, we all lived in an unrepentant, sinful state. During that time, our soul, the immaterial and eternal part of who we are, was controlled by our fleshly nature. The driving force behind all our actions and behaviors was rooted in sin and selfishness. The flesh dictated our inclinations, desires, behaviors, and actions. Simply put, the flesh initiated the behaviors, and our soul carried them out.

I vividly recall my attitudes and thought processes before fully surrendering my life to Christ. My entire mindset was contrary to God and His Word. What's worse, I considered myself a Christian and believed I would go to Heaven if I died. However, my heart, mind, and soul were directed by my flesh rather than God. The Bible teaches us that God is love, yet I lacked love for others and myself during those years. I remember a conversation I had one day when someone expressed concern about a stranger they believed was unsaved and destined for Hell. My response was callous: "Why should you care? You don't know them."

Today, that attitude feels foreign to me. When God transformed my life, I shifted from self-centeredness to genuinely loving and caring for total strangers. I am grateful God has given me countless opportunities to minister to, love, and fellowship with unknown individuals. While we may lack the ability to change ourselves, God can and will transform us if we allow Him.

This necessary transformation can only come from God; it is not something we can manufacture through self-will, determination, or resolve. We simply do not possess enough personal strength or resolve to bring about the change needed for the present and the future. We will delve into how this transformation occurs and what it means for us later. For now, however, I want us to reflect on our lives.

Changed

Day 2 Exercises

1. List the areas of your life that you are dissatisfied with.

___

2. Why are you dissatisfied with those areas?

___

3. How have you sought God's guidance to change these areas?

___

4. What would each of these areas look like if they were fully surrendered to God?

___

DAY 3
SELF-MADE

> *Proverbs 26:12*
>
> *"Do you see a person wise in their own eyes? There is more hope for a fool than for them."*

If you have completed Day 1 and Day 2 exercises, you should have identified areas of your life that have been out of sync with God. Prayerfully, you have been actively seeking to surrender those areas to the Lord and allowing Him to guide you. Our Scripture today reminds us that those who believe they are wise in and of themselves are even more foolish than a fool. Those self-made and wise in their own eyes will never achieve what they desire and ultimately will be worse off than they have ever imagined.

No one likes being humbled; whether we admit it or not, most of us deal with a bit of pride. We are taught at a young age to make something of ourselves, to take care of number one, and to take responsibility for our lives. These ideals sound good, and many who have applied these concepts to their lives have gone on to do and accomplish "great things," but it is not what God desires.

These sound-good traps are used to pull us away from God's plan and design. The most ridiculous aspect is that these same traps occur in religious matters. If you have read my book, "Promise Land, Exile to Redemption," you know that God had to demolish me to use me. I admit I fell into the self-made wisdom trap in some Spiritual matters.

I knew God had called me to the ministry, and at this time, I had answered that call. Somewhere in my first years, I began to formulate things I could do to make myself more called, righteous, and holy. I began to exchange the freedom of a relationship with the Lord for a set of religious rules. My Bible reading and prayer time went from enjoyable and productive to controlled and timed. I reached a point where I felt God couldn't use me unless I prayed, studied at least two and half hours a day, and fasted one to two days a week. In my own wisdom, I decided I had to tithe my time and desires to God.

As the Bible says, "There is more hope for a fool" than those who use their own wisdom. When God finished disciplining me, I was broken and confused. Amid God's humbling was where I finally realized I had been prideful. In the midst of "serving God," "sacrificing," and "pursuing righteousness," I had stopped being obedient and was guilty of being wise in my own eyes.

As we looked at "Needing A Change," most of our focus was on the areas where we have struggled and have had problems. Today, we should address the areas that we feel we have had under control. In doing so, we will probably find many of the same underlying driving forces that brought about our "problem areas" are active and present in almost all areas of our lives. Remember, we must get to the root of who we are and what we do if we are ever going to allow God to make the changes He desires.

Changed

Day 3 Exercises

1. Look at Day One's list of satisfied areas of your life, circle the ones you feel you've done a great job of accomplishing, and list them below.

   _____
   _____
   _____
   _____
   _____
   _____
   _____
   _____

2. Are the driving forces behind those satisfied areas pleasing to God? Explain why or why not.

   _____
   _____
   _____
   _____
   _____
   _____
   _____
   _____
   _____
   _____

3. What would be different about your life if all your motives and driving forces were to please and honor God?

   _____
   _____
   _____
   _____
   _____
   _____
   _____
   _____

3. Describe a God-made life verses a self-made life.

   _____
   _____
   _____
   _____
   _____
   _____
   _____
   _____

DAY 4

MY WAY

> *Proverbs 14:12*
>
> *"There is a way that seems right to a man, But its end is the way of death. (NKJV)*

Most of us have lived according to what seemed right to us. The problem is that our knowledge, understanding, and insight are limited by many factors. Everything we do, think, and feel emotionally is impacted by all the driving forces that have formed us from birth. If that were not limiting enough, our own experiences dictate what we believe to be real, factual, and accurate. When we factor in that our flesh nature rules almost everything we do, it is no wonder our ways lead to death.

From the moment we enter the world, we are taught and told what can and can't happen. These experiences and limitations simply equate to our inability to fathom the truth that God can do anything. Life has limited our understanding that God is not bound by the natural. He isn't limited by physics or hindered by human limitations. God is supernatural. In our world, two plus two equals four; this math is undeniable and unchangeable in the physical world. These natural laws add to why we lack the faith to believe God can change us. Life has made us ignorant of God's ability to intervene on our behalf. Too often, we fail to recognize God has proven time and time again throughout history that He is not limited by the natural limitations of this world, our understanding, or even our flesh nature.

One of my favorite passages which describes God's power over the natural comes from Matthew 14. In this passage, Jesus takes five loaves of bread and two fish and feeds 5,000 men, not including the women and the children that were present. If that were not miraculous enough, even though He only started with five loaves of bread (probably the size of biscuits) and two fish (likely no larger than sardines), once Jesus blessed it and broke it, the leftovers filled 12 baskets. This alone should be enough to encourage us that no matter what we face, God can and will reveal His perfect ways to us that lead to life.

In my life, there have been many times I thought I knew exactly what needed to happen. In fact, I was so confident that my planning was so accurate I didn't even consult God or ask what He desired. Each time I took the reins, the results were disastrous and always the opposite of what I desired to achieve. In my younger years, when I was living solely by the flesh, a friend and I went out and had been partying. I was past my curfew, and I let him drive us since he knew a shortcut home. That best thinking cost me a car, three months in a hospital bed, four months in a wheelchair, and another three months on crutches. "There is a way that seems right to a man, but its end is the way of death." My futile understanding, flesh nature, and driving forces from within put me in the situation in the first place. Then one bad decision after the other sealed my fate. I wouldn't have survived the accident that night short of God's grace. God is all-knowing, and despite my "right way of thinking," He spared me. I don't doubt that you have similar stories of when your "right thinking" should have cost you your life, yet God spared you. God did not give you this opportunity to waste away doing it your way. God is all-knowing. He sees in you what you don't even know is there. He knows the potential, the freedom, and the victory that He has prepared and is ready to bestow it upon you. Take courage and strength that what you have not been able to do, our Great, Sovereign, and Loving God can.

Changed

Day 4 Exercises

1. List some thought processes that have seemed right to you, but have been disastrous instead.

_____
_____
_____
_____
_____
_____
_____

2. Objectively describe the difference between what you have thought is right compared to what God's Word says is right.

_____
_____
_____
_____
_____
_____
_____
_____
_____
_____

3. From the thought processes listed in question 1, describe how you have tried to change them.

_____
_____
_____
_____
_____
_____
_____
_____

4. Why do you think you have failed to significantly impact these problem areas?

_____
_____
_____
_____
_____
_____
_____
_____

DAY 5

PLANTING

> *Galatians 6:8*
>
> *"Whoever sows to please their flesh, from the flesh will reap destruction; whoever sows to please the Spirit, from the Spirit will reap eternal life."*

We've been discussing the flesh nature and how it has controlled our thinking. The flesh nature itself is rooted in carnal pride and lust. The flesh always desires that which is contrary to God. Living to please our sinful, flesh nature brings us destruction, death, and turmoil. Most of us have a heap of destructive consequences we have amassed from living to please ourselves. I want to address the fact that these negative consequences are not limited to obvious destructive behaviors like substance use, sexual sins, anger, or even arrogance. We must remember our enemy, the one who drives the lust of this world and the lust of our flesh, doesn't care if we are bound in substance use or materialism. He only desires for us to be drawn more to the things of this world than to God. The enemy is satisfied if we are drowning in debt, running wild, or trapped in addiction.

In my twenties, I struggled with alcohol but was able to give it to God and experience deliverance. In my surrender, I felt drawn to ministry. I desired to serve God and be used by Him. The more I sought God, the more He spoke to me. One day while in prayer, the Lord took me to a passage of Scripture that verified God's call on my life, or at least I interpreted it that way. 1 Timothy 6:11-12 states, "But you, man of God, flee from all this, and pursue righteousness, godliness, faith, love, endurance, and gentleness. Fight the good fight of the faith. Take hold of the eternal life to which you were called when you made your good confession in the presence of many witnesses." I was so excited, I felt as though God Himself was giving me His approval; after all, He said… "but you man of God…". I held on to that verse internally, knowing that God saw my faith, love, and endurance and that He approved. Yes, I was being ridiculous. While relishing in my interpretation of the Scripture, I failed to surrender other areas of my life. I knew drinking didn't honor God, and I had stopped that. I was working hard, paying my bills, attending church, and being a "man of God," or so I thought.

To shorten my ten-year side-track, I was doing well at my job and felt I could and should have nice things. So I began buying cars, motorcycles, trucks, boats, computers, stereo equipment, clothes, and anything else I thought I would like. I spent way more than I was making, so credit cards became the answer. Before I knew it, I was in so much debt I had to work even more hours just to try and keep up. Church fell by the wayside, and somehow, just a few short years after being affirmed as a "man of God," I was financially ruined, broken spiritually and emotionally, and wondered how I got into this mess. In the midst of all this, God took me back to the verse He had given me. This time the words "man of God" didn't stick out. What captured my attention was "flee from all this." I began to question what "this" was and read the verses above. 1 Timothy 6:6-10, "But godliness with contentment is great gain. For we brought nothing into the world, and we can take nothing out of it. But if we have food and clothing, we will be content with that. Those who want to get rich fall into temptation and a trap and into many foolish and harmful desires that plunge people into ruin and destruction. For the love of money is the root of all kinds of evil. Some people, eager for money, have wandered from the faith and pierced themselves with many griefs." I realized that God was warning me, but unfortunately I had ignored Him. Today, no matter where you are in your walk with God, understand He desires the best for you. The world will offer you many things, some of which will bring temporary pleasure, but eventually they all lead to a path of destruction. Seek the things of God, and you will find that abundant life you desire.

Changed

Day 5 Exercises

1. What specific seeds have I been planting that lead to destruction?

_____
_____
_____
_____
_____
_____
_____
_____

2. What specific seeds have I been planting that lead to eternal life?

_____
_____
_____
_____
_____
_____
_____
_____

3. List specific seeds that God desires you to plant.

_____
_____
_____
_____
_____
_____
_____

4. Write a Bible verse that you have held on to that gives you hope and encouragement.

_____
_____
_____
_____
_____
_____
_____

DAY 6
FAMILY TRAITS

> *Numbers 14:18*
>
> *"The LORD is slow to anger and filled with unfailing love, forgiving every kind of sin and rebellion. But he does not excuse the guilty. He lays the sins of the parents upon their children; the entire family is affected even children in the third and fourth generations."*

Many of us have battled repeatedly with the same circumstances and issues our parents and grandparents fought to overcome. Some of these battles have seemed to engulf entire families, with almost every living family member being trapped in the same behaviors. Many have suggested traits like alcoholism and addiction are passed down to us genetically. However, the Bible declares there are sins that affect the entire family and that certain sins are passed down through generations. Addiction may be the easiest generational sin to identify, but there are many more. Some examples of generational sins are financial struggles, relationship issues, divorce, abuse, and even some mental and emotional health issues. As you can see, the areas potentially affected by our ancestors are virtually endless. The reality is that any sinful behavior or mindset could be from a generational sin. Examining your family lineage is the easiest way to determine if you're dealing with a generational sin or not. If you see the same destructive patterns within the same family line, then the issue very well may be a generational sin.

Examining my own life and looking at my family revealed a generational sin of divorce. Interestingly enough, my grandparents and great-grandparents were not part of this, as they were only ever married once and remained married to their spouses until they died. Nonetheless, among my uncle, mother, father, and brother, it seemed that divorce had attached itself to our family. My uncle had been divorced three times, my mother four, my father five, and my brother three times. I knew without asking the Lord to break this curse over my family that I was headed in the same direction. Through prayer, that generational sin was broken over my family, and we have been delivered from it.

I would like to point out that, somehow, divorce attached itself to my family. Remember, my grandparents were never divorced. I draw attention to this because generational sins can start at any time and come from any individual. Remember, the sins of the fathers are passed down to the third and fourth generations. This spirit of divorce could have begun with unknown infidelity generations before. My point is, our actions, what we do, how we act, and the sins we permit in our life will not only affect us but could potentially affect our great-great-great-grandchildren. This is why allowing God to deliver us and set us free is so important.

So far this week, we have been taking a hard look at ourselves and seeking to find out what got us in our mess in the first place. We have looked at the insanity of our lives. We have seen the passage from Romans play out within us repeatedly, doing what we don't want to do and ultimately not doing what we want to do. Looking at our thought processes, we should conclude that our best thinking has been absolutely foolish. In addition, we should have realized everything we thought was best and right has left a path of destruction and unforeseen consequences. Reaching this point and surrendering to the fact that it will take an act of God to change us is precisely where we need to be. Recognizing our need for Divine intervention and surrendering our will is the beginning of finding the "New You."

Changed

Day 6 Exercises

1. List sins and behaviors that have been present in your family lines.

___

2. How has your life been unmanageable?

___

3. Describe what your life would look like free from these generational sins.

___

4. Write out a prayer asking God to break each specific generational sin.

___

DAY 7
DESERVING DEATH

> *Ephesians 2:3*
>
> *"All of us also lived among them at one time, gratifying the cravings of our flesh and following its desires and thoughts. Like the rest, we were by nature deserving of wrath."*

Many people seem to believe they are good people, willing to help others and desiring no harm to come upon anyone else. Even though they might be known as the kind of individual who would give you the shirt off their back, while admirable, it doesn't make them right with God. According to God's Word, none are righteous. The truth is that all of us have lived to satisfy and gratify our flesh nature and have fallen short of God's glory. No matter how we try to dress ourselves up with good deeds, our flesh nature is contrary to God and opposes His will. Our passage today clearly states that all who follow the desires and thoughts of the flesh deserve God's wrath.

God's wrath is eternal separation from Him; this is what Hell is: a place of torment, a lake of fire that can't be put out, and an eternal existence with no hope of God's presence ever being manifested. This place was created and reserved for the devil and his demons. It was never made for you and me. God loves us so much and desires for us to abide with Him for eternity that He provided everything we need to find Him and receive eternal life. The truth is, God doesn't send anyone to Hell. If we remain unrepentant, unchanged, and stuck in the flesh nature, it is because we have chosen to do so. God can't do any more to save us; He has already done everything necessary. Plainly put, if you are distant from God, stuck in the ways of the flesh, struggling to find hope, or overwhelmed with sin, it is because you choose to do so. Now you may not wake up each and every day and consciously decide to remain bound in sin, but each day you don't allow God to take control, that is what you are doing. There have been times when I felt stuck and unable to make the necessary changes to improve my life. In those times, I came up with all kinds of excuses, but everything changed when I finally quit making excuses and decided to do it God's way. This is true for socially acceptable behaviors and life-controlling sins that need deliverance.

My weight was the area I made the most excuses. As a teenager, I was always heavier than my classmates, which continued well into adulthood. My battle with obesity extended well beyond finding salvation, sobriety, and purpose. Even as a pastor who faithfully served God, my weight was out of control. I made all the excuses about my metabolism, being big-boned and even joked that God just made me this way. But, the truth is I had areas of my life that were controlled by the flesh and not the Spirit.

When I finally surrendered my eating habits to the Lord, faithfully exercised, and ate responsibly, I began to lose weight. God had provided a way for my weight to be under control all these years, but I just hadn't received it. We will change when we finally recognize that no excuses exist for our lives to remain controlled by the flesh. Finding freedom won't be us changing but instead surrendering to the will of God and His nature. There is no sin, no lifestyle of satisfying the flesh, and no defeat in Him. In Christ, there is only victory and freedom. Learning to live by God's nature and not the flesh nature won't feel natural, but when we get through it, we won't recognize the individual looking back at us in the mirror. Regardless of the sacrifice, the transformed life God has promised us is worth it all. The best part is not just the deliverance we experience but the restored relationship we have with God.

Changed

Day 7 Exercises

1. Without a right relationship with God, what is my expected end?

_____
_____
_____
_____
_____
_____
_____
_____

2. What specific things (desires, sins, ect.) must I surrender to have a right relationship with God?

_____
_____
_____
_____
_____
_____
_____
_____
_____

3. What is God's plan for me as an individual?

_____
_____
_____
_____
_____
_____
_____
_____

4. Write in your own words a summary of all that we have discussed this week.

_____
_____
_____
_____
_____
_____
_____
_____

Week 2

> *"I can't fix, change or even better myself but the One who created me can."*

Last week's devotionals clarified that we are the root cause of our inability to change. We, our abilities, reasoning, and understanding, put our lives in the mess they are in now. To think that we can muster enough determination and resolve to make an effective change is ridiculous, considering we couldn't keep ourselves from succumbing to those spiritual, genetic, and emotional influences that molded and shaped us in the first place. Having come to this understanding and knowing effective change is out of our control, we must take the next necessary step if we are ever going to become who God designed us to be.

Within the 12 steps, the next step in recovery is to believe that God, who is the One more powerful than us, can restore us to sanity and stability. Recognizing a life of purpose, recovery, and change is not only out of our control but isn't in our ability, nor our responsibility is what prepares us for victory. Understanding that change is out of our control, we must ask, "Who is in control?" The answer is God. God is the One who is able, capable, and responsible for fixing what sin has broken within us. Only the One who created us can know us intimately and intricately enough to know precisely how to restore us to our intended state.

I encourage you to take a moment and review the answers to the questions in Week One with the mindset that you have been living the life the world dealt to you. So many of the things you've been through, choices you've made, and behaviors you've exhibited have actually been out of your control. Hopefully, you can understand why it always seemed that no matter how hard you tried to change, you always ended up returning to the same old things. Your inability to create change explains the insanity of doing the same thing over and over again, expecting different results.

Prayerfully you are now finally ready and able to forgive yourself. You did not ruin your life, nor did you solely choose to be where and who you are today. Sin, the flesh nature, genetics, trauma, spiritual laws, and environmental influences have all contributed to your mess. You cannot cure sin, defeat the flesh nature, change your genetics, remove the effects of trauma, redefine spiritual laws, nor change the impact of environmental influences. Only God can fix, heal, change, and redefine all that has defined you. Blaming and condemning yourself for that which is out of your control is counterproductive to becoming who God created you to be.

Changed

Take these newfound freedoms and forgiveness and use them to run to God. Until now, most of us have been running from God because of our shame and guilt. I want you to know that He loves you more than you could ever think or imagine. Our God has a deep desire to heal and forgive you. In fact, He longs so much for each of us to be with Him that He has done everything necessary for us to find healing and forgiveness. However, I do want you to understand we don't get a free pass from the consequences of sin, even if most of the things that have made us who we are today have been out of our control.

Even so, we will all be held accountable for the sin in our lives. This accountability will include all of those underlying driving forces in our lives we didn't create along with every decision, thought, and action we are responsible for. God desires to forgive us, and He is the only One who can change us. His mercy means we are free to forgive ourselves for ending up the way we are. This freedom is not a license to remain unchanged or even permission to continue to live a life contrary to God's Word; no, we will answer to God. The penalty will be paid for every sinful behavior and choice we have made. God will hold us accountable. After all, God Himself made a way for our sins to be paid. He paved the way to a transformed life, and He has promised to create us as brand new beings, free from sin and its effects.

We may not have been able to choose what we battle or how the flesh nature dictates our behaviors, but we can choose whether or not we will surrender to God. If we remain unchanged, stuck, and controlled by sinful desires, it is because we choose to do so. Let that sink in for a moment. You remain who you are because you choose to do so. You remain bound by addiction, controlled by desires, and stuck in your ways because you choose to. God can do nothing more than He has already done to set you free. When Christ said on the cross, "It is finished," everything necessary for our freedom and deliverance was complete. (John 19:30) As we move forward in Week 2, approach each day with the mindset that you can't do anything on your own; you need God's help in order to change. The Good News is, God has already done everything necessary for your freedom.

DAY 8

GOD CAN DO IT

> *Matthew 19:25-26*
>
> *"²⁵ When the disciples heard this... they asked "Who then can be saved?" ²⁶ Jesus looked at them and said, "With man this is impossible, but with God all things are possible."*

At Promise Land, we have a saying, "A saved life is a changed life." This statement states that you can't experience salvation without being changed. In today's passage, the disciples ask Jesus, "Who then can be saved?" Jesus' answer to them explains why we haven't been able to make the necessary changes in our own lives. His answer simply states that obtaining salvation in our own ability is impossible. The truth is, we can't change ourselves, and we can't be good enough to save ourselves. We are dependent upon God to save us and change us. It really does take a Power greater than ourselves to break the insanity and instability of our lives. Before we get too much further in our devotionals, we must address what a saved life is. Many who have picked this devotional up are seeking to change specific destructive behaviors. They think that if they can only stop the things that are driving their lives to be out of control, they will be fine. Unfortunately, this is not true. The problem is not the destructive behavior. The problem that each of us has is an incorrect relationship with God. The destructive behaviors are an effect of a broken relationship with God. So when we say "saved," we are not talking about being saved from addiction or other specific behaviors.

The term "saved" means to be delivered from the penalty of sin. That penalty is eternal death. This death is not a one-time experience but instead is eternal separation from God in a lake of eternal fire called Hell. To be saved means to be born again. If you have read my book "Created," then you have a good understanding of what it means to be born again. For a quick review, when we surrender our lives to Christ and accept Him as our Lord and Savior, we are born again; Christ's death on the cross becomes the payment for the penalty of our sins. Having this debt paid means we are saved. When we experience the miracle of salvation, all those spiritual things that formed us within the womb are broken, and we receive a new spiritual DNA, so to speak, and become who and what God designed us to be.

It should be easy to see why all of this is impossible for man. We cannot pay our own debt; God must. We cannot save ourselves; God must. We cannot recreate and redefine our existence; God must, and because He is God, nothing is impossible for Him. Only God can restore us. Only God can take us from our instability and plant us on His Word's solid and unshakeable foundation. Remember, we said that a saved life is a changed life. In my personal experience, I grew up in the church. In fact, both of my grandfathers were ministers. I had grown up in church and had knowledge of who Jesus is, the price He paid for my sin, and the fact that He rose from the dead. I knew it in my head and accepted it to be true. But, unfortunately, knowing it in my head and living a life that proves I believe Him to be my Lord and Savior are two different things.

It wasn't until way into my adulthood did I realize I needed to know the Lord in my heart for myself, not just to know all about Him in my head. When I finally realized this and answered His call unto salvation, I was transformed, born again, delivered, and set free from the sin that had captured me. Not only did God empower me to overcome the destructive behaviors I had been trapped in, but He restored me to a right relationship with Him that has guided and directed me in everything since. Who I was changed; I didn't just stop doing something; He transformed me.

Changed

Day 8 Exercises

1. In what ways have I tried to save myself?

2. Why have my best efforts failed?

3. What would a transformed (born again) life look like?

4. Write out a prayer asking God to change you.

DAY 9

TOUCHING JESUS

> *Luke 8:43-44*
>
> *"⁴³ And a woman was there who had been subject to bleeding for twelve years…but no one could heal her. ⁴⁴ She came up behind him and touched the edge of his cloak, and immediately her bleeding stopped."*

In today's passage, the woman spoken of here had an issue with bleeding for twelve years. It says she had spent all her money on physicians, but no one could heal her. I don't know about you, but I feel that this describes the condition of a lot of us. We have tried all the traditional routes to fix what is wrong with us. So many of us have tried expensive programs, bought every self-help book on the subject, and tried everything from physicians to ancient remedies, only to still be plagued by the same issues. This woman tried everything, and nothing worked. She was desperate! In her desperation, she heard about a man who had the power to heal. She had heard the rumors that He was a great Prophet, an excellent Teacher, and maybe even the Son of God, the long-awaited Messiah. In her desperation, she came to believe that what Jesus had done for others, He could do for her. Somewhere in her heart, she concluded she would be healed if she could just touch Jesus. When she arrived, a huge crowd surrounded Jesus, and He must have seemed unattainable to her.

According to the Old Testament, anyone with an issue of blood was considered unclean. Anything they touched would be unclean, and anyone who touched them or that they had touched would be unclean. This woman had been unclean for twelve years. She would have been barred from the temple and would have had to announce that she was unclean whenever in public. She became desperate and determined, believing Jesus could heal her. She was willing to do whatever it took to reach Him. She didn't care what people thought. She didn't care what they would say. She didn't care if she was disliked. She had reached the very place that we all must reach if we are ever going to be healed, a place where we are ready and willing to do whatever it takes to touch Jesus, knowing that when we do, we will be healed. How we reach out and touch Him may differ for each of us, but make no mistake, real freedom will only come once we do. I didn't have an issue of blood, but I did have problems. My biggest problem was that I didn't think I had a problem. I thought I was okay, that my decisions and life choices were permissible, and I felt that I wasn't that bad especially compared to some people. The issue for me was I could always find someone way worse than me to make myself feel better about what I was doing. In case you don't know this yet, we are not to compare ourselves to other lost people or even those who may be born again. If we want to measure ourselves to see how we stack up, we must compare ourselves to Jesus.

The moment I finally recognized my way wasn't working was when I lost everything and was left all alone. I was in the middle of an ice storm with it freezing cold outside, and I was in a barn apartment with no heat. I was sitting in that apartment all by myself, broke, broken, and hopeless, my teeth were chattering, and I was shivering, trying to get under enough blankets to stay warm. At that moment, I started questioning how I got into this situation and why I had let myself go so far from what I had been taught. It was there that Christ revealed Himself to me, and it was there that I realized what had put me in this situation in the first place. It wasn't a habit, a person, or even the particulars of the current events that got me where I was. No, my conscious decisions to live my life according to my best thinking put me in that position. I realized that my best thinking and reasoning would always take me down the same road again and again and that only by surrendering to the Lord could I find freedom.

Changed

Day 9 Exercises

1. What will it take for you to reach out to Jesus?

_____
_____
_____
_____
_____
_____
_____

2. How will what others (including friends and family) say affect your decision to surrender to Christ?

_____
_____
_____
_____
_____
_____
_____
_____

3. What has been your biggest problem?

_____
_____
_____
_____
_____
_____
_____
_____

4. Write a detailed response on how to fix your biggest problem.

_____
_____
_____
_____
_____
_____
_____
_____

DAY 10
CHANGE OF HEART

> *Ezekiel 36:26*
>
> *"And I will give you a new heart, and I will put a new spirit in you. I will take out your stony, stubborn heart and give you a tender, responsive heart." (NLT)*

At this point, we should all be clear we can't change ourselves and it will take God intervening in our lives in order to see any real, lasting change. With that realization, we should know we must come to God to find freedom. As we learned in yesterday's devotional, we know that we should come to God by faith in anticipation and with the expectation that once we go to Jesus, we will be healed and delivered.

Today's passage shares God's promise to give us a new heart and a new Spirit. This is what happens when we are saved, that is, born again. God is not interested in just adjusting our behaviors. He is not interested in just fixing the areas we deem to be broken, nor is He interested in making us "good" people. The truth is, God desires to transform us totally. Our passage today doesn't say He will soften our hearts; no, it says He will give us a new heart. It is from our hearts that all of our desires, thoughts, and actions derive. His promise of a new heart is a promise to change our entire identity. Even beyond this transformation, God has also promised to give us a new Spirit. Receiving a new Spirit speaks to removing the flesh nature and replacing it with His nature. Having God's Spirit living in and through us will be what guides us and directs us to all He has designed for us. His Spirit in us will be what takes that "stony, stubborn heart" that has allowed our flesh to dictate all we do and replace it with a "tender, responsive heart." In other words, we will be changed from being unresponsive to God, His love, and His plan to being open, ready, and willing to respond and obey His direction.

Still to this day, I remember the attitude I had years ago, long before I got right with God. My attitude was cold, stubborn, and selfish. It surely didn't reflect Christ or His love and concern for all. I remember an individual that was crying over a stranger. I remember asking them what was wrong and why they seemed so concerned about someone they didn't know. Their response took me back; they said they thought the person might go to Hell. I remember thinking to myself that I didn't know them and that I didn't care. The truth was, at that stage of my life, I didn't love myself, much less anybody else. Verbalizing my feelings made me stop and think about where I was in my walk with the Lord. I realized my behaviors and actions didn't match who I said I was. For example, I declared that I was saved and that I was a disciple of Christ, yet the Scriptures state that "God is love," and I didn't love anyone. It also says in John 13:35, "By this everyone will know that you are my disciples if you love one another." I came face to face with the fact that I was living a lie. The truth was, I was only lying to myself. I had deceived myself into believing I was okay with God, that I was saved and belonged to Him.

The reality was my heart was cold and hard. How I lived my life proved that His Spirit didn't live in me. We must all reach a point when we face the truth that once God moves in, we are changed. Our cold, bitter, and selfish heart ruled by the flesh nature is removed. When God gives us His heart, His Spirit, and His love, we are changed, transformed, and born again. If you're walking through life knowing in your head that Jesus is the Son of God, Lord, and Savior, but your actions, behavior, and compassion show you are still ruling your own life, you should question if you have been saved. Knowing Him in your head and living a life that declares you are His are two very different things. We won't be judged for what we know, but we will answer for what we do.

Changed

Day 10 Exercises

1. List the attributes or behaviors of your life that do not line up with a tender, responsive heart filled with God's Spirit.

_____
_____
_____
_____
_____
_____
_____
_____

2. To the best of your ability explain how God feels about those behaviors.

_____
_____
_____
_____
_____
_____
_____
_____

3. Do you consider yourself saved?

_____
_____
_____
_____
_____
_____
_____
_____

4. What behaviors, thoughts or patterns are in your life that do not verify you have been saved?

_____
_____
_____
_____
_____
_____
_____
_____

DAY 11

FREE

> *John 8:34-36*
>
> *"³⁴ Jesus replied, "Very truly I tell you, everyone who sins is a slave to sin. ³⁵ Now a slave has no permanent place in the family, but a son belongs to it forever. ³⁶ So if the Son sets you free, you will be free indeed."*

Whether we know it or not, we all have been slaves to sin. Each of us has been controlled and mastered by our flesh nature to some extent. Even now, you still may not have fully surrendered to the Lord and received His nature. Today's passage again clarifies that there are only two states or conditions we can be in, slave to sin or free. The passage states, "Everyone who sins is a slave to sin... if the Son sets you free, you are free indeed." Working through this devotional should help you recognize that we are either enslaved by sin or free, saved or unsaved, right or wrong, forgiven or unforgiven, born again or still the same, Heaven bound or Hell bound.

We must realize that there is no middle ground. There is no spiritual place where we live in our sinful flesh nature and are right with God. There is no being saved and enslaved, no living for self and serving God. Reaching this realization is paramount if we expect any lasting change. The enemy would have us believe we can be ok with God and live in the ways of the world. God's word is clear about how He feels about sin, compromise, and those who live to satisfy the "lust of the flesh, the lust of the eyes and the pride of life." (John 2:16). In the verse before this, it states: "Do not love the world or anything in the world. If anyone loves the world, the love of the Father is not in him." There simply is no way to love the world or the things of the world and love God. If we feel or believe otherwise, we have deceived ourselves, and we will find ourselves in a terrible spot on the day we are called to give an account before our Lord.

In contrast, those who have been born again are free. This freedom is a release from the control of the flesh nature. It is being set free from the penalty of sin and gives us the freedom to live a righteous and blameless life. You may have heard the expression, "you're either a Saint or an ain't." This summarizes the reality of there being no middle ground and shows us our need to seek the Lord and accept His help so we can live the holy life we are called to live. I know just how easy it is to live in that non-existent middle ground. Having been raised in the church, I knew all about the Lord and how to say just the right things. I could quote Scripture and even lead someone to the Lord using Scripture passages. Unfortunately, as you have already read, I wasn't living what I was saying. My heart did not desire to be obedient to God; in, I was only concerned with what I needed. I wasn't a bad guy, so to speak. I wasn't robbing or stealing, or physically hurting anyone. Yet the flesh controlled me, and I was a slave to sin and selfishness. What made matters worse was I thought I was saved. I had said the sinners' prayer at a young age and had a brief moment of behavior adjustment. Unfortunately, the changes I had made were made in my own strength, and before I knew it, I was back to the same old selfish lifestyle.

The Good News is, no matter how long we have been enslaved by sin, controlled by the flesh, or stuck in our behaviors, we can be set free by Jesus. Once set free by Jesus, we are delivered, transformed, and totally changed. Today's Scripture sums it up for us (I hope you catch it) it states: "If the Son sets you free, you will be free indeed." You will be free indeed, which means it is sure, absolute, and unquestionable. If the Son of God, Jesus Christ, transforms you, then you will be free. Those set free don't waiver back and forth, they don't backslide into the same old behaviors, and they don't say one thing and do another.

Changed

Day 11 Exercises

1. What behaviors have you been enslaved to?

_____
_____
_____
_____
_____
_____
_____

2. Explain why it is impossible to be set free and remain enslaved.

_____
_____
_____
_____
_____
_____
_____

3. What do you feel the Lord needs to do for you to be set free?

_____
_____
_____
_____
_____
_____
_____

4. What is stopping you from being completely free?

_____
_____
_____
_____
_____
_____
_____

DAY 12

SOMETHING NEW

> *2 Corinthians 5:17*
>
> *"Therefore, if anyone is in Christ, the new creation has come: The old has gone, the new is here!"*

We have seen that freedom can only be found in and through Jesus. Freedom isn't changing or adjusting destructive behaviors or even replacing bad habits with good habits. Freedom goes beyond the changing of behaviors; freedom is being totally released from sin and its penalty. Those that are in Christ are transformed into a new creation. This new creation isn't a patched-up version of your old self. It is a brand new you, made without all those broken and corrupt things that once dictated who you were. The more we study God's Word, the more we understand that God works in absolutes. In plain words, God said it, and it happened. It didn't almost happen or kind of happen; all that God said came to be. This is how it works: God speaks, and what He speaks comes to be. In the beginning, God said let there be light, and light, which never existed before, came to be. The whole creation account in Genesis verifies what God speaks comes to pass. This fact is not limited to just creation, as it can be clearly seen throughout the Old and New Testaments. We see those Jesus healed and set free were changed completely and permanently. Paul never struggled and went back to hunting down and killing Christians. The lame man didn't relapse and struggle with an inability to walk.

If we struggle with overcoming particular sins, behaviors, or anything else, it is because we haven't been transformed or we've chosen to remain stuck in them. Choosing to remain in them happens for one of two reasons. We either don't want to give them up, desiring our flesh nature over the freedom God has offered, or we simply do not believe God can be trusted. Either way, it is time to comprehend that we can't be born again, transformed and re-created, all the while staying the same; that is impossible! I've shared that I lived for years believing I was saved and born again. I am unsure how I believed it as my life was far from transformed. I was living to please myself and had no interest in pleasing God. In Revelation 3:15-16, we read, "I know all the things you do, that you are neither hot nor cold. I wish that you were one or the other! But since you are like lukewarm water, neither hot nor cold, I will spit you out of my mouth!" I was living a lukewarm life. My actions and behaviors were not bad by the world's standards, but they weren't in line with God's. Honestly, it would have been better if I had been bad enough to obviously know I needed transformation, rather than living deceived.

I lived a self-deceived life for years, but I will never forget the day God got my attention, and I realized I lacked the transformation that comes from being born again. It was a Sunday morning, and I had taken the day off of work to see my brother get baptized. He had a brief moment where he went to church and decided to surrender to the Lord. I went to the service expecting to see my brother, but he didn't show up. After the service, the congregation visited a nearby city park for a river baptism. I watched as individuals walked forward, grabbed the Pastor's hand, and walked out into the water about waist-deep. Each one who came forward shared a short testimony and was baptized. After the last one had been baptized, the Pastor asked if anyone present needed to get their baptism in order. He said we shouldn't waste another day, and if God was speaking to us, we should answer. I couldn't shake it. God was speaking to me like never before. He revealed to me how far I was from Him. He reminded me of the call to the ministry He had placed on my life and asked me how long I would do it my way. I was broken. The weight and the reality of my selfish and sinful lifestyle was more than I could handle. I asked God to forgive me as I tossed my wallet and phone to the ground. I walked out, grabbed the Pastor's hand, and told everyone I was tired of living my life my way. I was ready to live solely for God. At that moment, I was transformed. The Pastor baptized me, and I haven't looked back since.

Changed

Day 12 Exercises

1. How have you been living against God's Word?

2. Explain why you do or why you don't feel that you are saved.

3. What would your life look like if God transformed you?

4. Explain why you are struggling with old behaviors if you have been transformed.

DAY 13
GOD GUIDES

> *Philippians 2:13*
>
> *"For God is working in you, giving you the desire and the power to do what pleases him."*

Every one of us has wants, dreams, and desires, all of which come from within. They are either driven by our old flesh nature or the new Spirit-filled nature we receive when born again. Our pre-transformed, flesh nature controlled all of what we did before surrendering to the Lord. We have seen how genetics, spiritual laws, and in-utero factors have dictated that old nature. Those factors lead us to actions and behaviors that, in and of themselves each had their own spiritual, physical, and emotional consequences. When born again, God replaces all that with His Spirit and gives us His nature. This releases us from being who we have always been and doing what we have always done because He makes us into a brand new creation. Our passage today explains it is not us who change our behaviors. It is not us who have to figure out what to do and how to do it. It is not us who have to recreate ourselves and change our desires. All of this is God's responsibility. It is only our responsibility to willingly allow God to do what He desires. Even after being transformed, born-again, and redefined, we still have free-will choice. God will never force us to do anything. He will not force us to change, nor will He force us to love Him. If we choose His will over self-will, He will change the very desires of our hearts. We will find a new, deep desire to do what pleases Him. What He desires for us is way greater than anything we can think or imagine. The biggest and best we have ever dreamed of doesn't compare to what God has planned for us. The last part of this passage stands out even more to me. It says that He will give us the power to do what pleases Him. We see this power displayed in Peter's life after his transformation.

Before receiving God's Spirit, Peter denied Christ. (Luke 22:54-62) In Peter's own strength and ability, he was unable to stand up publicly for Jesus. He said no when confronted about being one of those who walked with Jesus. He didn't do this once, but three times. In and of himself, Peter could not do that which God desired of him. The same is true for us. In our power, understanding, and ability, we will never be able to fulfill what God desires for us. Once Peter received God's Spirit, this all changed. We read in Acts 2 of the Holy Spirit descending upon Peter and empowering him as promised by Jesus. This empowerment enabled Peter to declare the truths of God publicly, and when he did, we are told that 5,000 men, not including women and children, accepted Christ as their Savior. This same man who could not identify as a disciple of Christ publicly, once transformed, was empowered to fulfill the desires of God.

When God transformed me, He empowered me to do what I could not do alone. I was unable to deliver myself. No matter how much I desired to change my ways, I always did the same old things repeatedly. I was trapped. No matter how sick and tired I was of suffering the consequences of my sins, I couldn't escape. The day I stepped into those baptismal waters, it all changed. God's Spirit came into me, and He began changing my desires. I don't struggle with doing the things I once desired to do. I now desire for my life to be a testimony for the Lord and to live a life that honors God. My flesh nature no longer controls me. From time to time, it does try to usurp authority, but with God's help, I can overcome it. This is the thing I want you to grasp for today's devotional: When we are saved, God's Spirit enters us, and as long as we are growing in our relationship with Him, the flesh nature is kept at bay. It is when our praying, Bible study, church-going, worshiping, and fellowshipping with other believers dwindles that flesh nature begins to regain control. The longer we allow our relationship with God to weaken, the more the flesh controls our lives. The greater our relationship with God, the more our lives are controlled by His Spirit.

Changed

Day 13 Exercises

1. What would your life look like if you had a great relationship with the Lord?

_____
_____
_____
_____
_____
_____
_____
_____

2. How can you improve your relationship with God?

_____
_____
_____
_____
_____
_____
_____
_____

3. List specific desires you have and identify if they are from the flesh or from God's Spirit.

_____
_____
_____
_____
_____
_____
_____
_____

4. What responsibility do you have in changing your desires?

_____
_____
_____
_____
_____
_____
_____

DAY 14
BROKEN CHAINS

> *Psalm 107:13-14*
>
> *"13 Lord, help!" they cried in their trouble, and he saved them from their distress. 14 He led them from the darkness and deepest gloom; He snapped their chains."*

Realizing that we cannot save ourselves and that we must have God help us is the beginning of freedom. Calling on Him for help is how freedom is obtained. Our passage today verifies this as it tells us to cry out for help in times of trouble, and the Lord will answer. He will save us from ourselves, our sins, and everything that has bound us up. Those feelings of despair and gloom which have made us feel hopeless and helpless are about to be changed. I like how the passage states that God is the One who will lead us from those feelings. This means to me that the situations are still there, and they may remain there, but God will lead us away. They will no longer hold power over us. Then, to top it all off, God Himself will snap our chains.

"Lord, help!" Those words are all that it takes. Those two words hold as much power as any hour-long prayer. Please pay attention; it isn't the words that set you free but the position of your heart, the desire for God's deliverance, and the willingness to receive His help. In Matthew 14:30, Peter prayed a similar prayer: "Lord, save me." His situation was dire. Peter had displayed His faith in the Lord and stepped out of the boat amid a storm. Then, like many of us, he began to look at the circumstances. He was overwhelmed when he saw the waves and the wind in the midst of the storm. Then, the thought that he was doing the impossible caused him to doubt, and that is all it took. That one moment was all it took for Peter to be overwhelmed by his known natural realities, and he started to sink. In his desperation, He cried out to the Lord, "Save me!" At that moment, Jesus reached out, grabbed his hand, and delivered him from his condition.

God will answer when we cry out to the Lord for help and truly mean it. All that had once trapped us, overwhelmed us, held control, and the flesh nature itself will no longer be able to enslave us. The world may be right that in the natural state of things, you may be unable to change, overcome addictions, break those generational curses, or escape the despair that engulfs you. In the natural, Peter would never have been able to walk on water. This is what we must realize: crying out to God for help is crying out to the One and only One who is above the natural. He is supernatural and, therefore, can do that which you nor anyone else can. He can grab your hand, come alongside you, and raise you out of all that has engulfed you. Walking with Him, you will overcome, and He will lead you out of all the storms of life.

I have watched many people say, "Lord, help" and "Lord, save me," but that is all they did; they just said the words. Going through the motions doesn't bring forth transformation. Taking the hand God extends to you, surrendering to His leadership, and walking through life with Him is what it takes. So, as we go through this 90-day journey, don't just go through the motions, but really and truly cry out to God for His help. Don't approach any of this journey with the focus or mindset of just being delivered from the consequences of your sin or being set free from a specific life-controlling problem. God isn't interested in stopping a habit or changing a specific behavior. He wants all of you and wants to transform every aspect of who you are. He desires to save you, not just save you from something. Remember, "those that the Son sets free are free indeed." Call on Him and watch him transform you from hopeless to hopeful, from turmoil to peace, and from chained to free.

Day 14 Exercises

1. What limitations do you have that are hindering your situation from changing?

___

2. What things have you accepted as normal, (family behaviors, attitudes, generational norms, etc.) that don't line up with God's word and His desires for you?

___

3. How have you seen God's power work in other peoples's lives?

___

4. What areas of your life do you feel need no change?

___

Week 3

> *"Every decision has a result, the result of surrendering to God is freedom."*

We know that God is the only One who can change us. The Bible states in Jeremiah 29:11, "'For I know the plans I have for you', declares the Lord, 'plans to prosper you and not to harm you, plans to give you hope and a future.'" This is God's desire for each of us. He longs to do what He has promised. His plan for us is to flourish and be prosperous, to live a life full of hope with the complete assurance we need, to have no fear of the future, resting in the fact He is in control. This means the life we have been living is not the one God designed for us. All it takes for us to find this God-designed life is to surrender our lives and will to Him. We will be born again, transformed, and saved when we do this.

In recovery, we must consciously decide to turn our will and lives over to God's care. In certain circles, they say "to god as you understand him." I would say, not as we understand, but as the Bible declares Him to be, the One true God. A god that we understand is a god that we have created, one confined by our knowledge, and turning our will and lives over to a god that we understand is to turn our lives back over to ourselves. We have always served a man-made god; we don't need "a god;" we need God. Isaiah 55:8 "For My thoughts are not your thoughts, neither are your ways My ways," declares the Lord." God's ways are not our ways. Remember, the natural does not limit Him because He is supernatural.

What you have not been able to figure out, He already knows. He can accomplish what you have been unable to because our God knows no limitations. The enemy would have you believe that God cannot be trusted, but God is the only One who is trustworthy. If we are going to be successful in recognizing the enemy's deception, we need to know how he works. The Good News is that he has been using the same old tricks since the beginning. The same deceptions he used in the Garden of Eden are the same deceptions he uses today. When we recognize what he is doing, it is much easier to reject the lies and turn our lives over to God's care.

The first deception the enemy used in the Garden was to create doubt about what God said. With Eve, the enemy asked, "Did God really say?" This was to create doubt about God's law, His requirements, and His direction. This tactic is still used today against us. If the enemy can get us to question what God's Word says, then he can begin to work doubt in our lives, and that doubt will lead to sin. Then the enemy uses our flesh nature and our natural desires for self-preservation to take us down the slippery slope of pride.

Changed

The devil tempted Eve, by saying, "You will be like God, knowing good from evil." This same temptation to be like God is prevalent today. Most of us wouldn't say we want to be God, but when we decide what we do, how we do it, and when we do it, we are placing ourselves as god of our own lives. Ultimately, this is pride, and pride is what got Satan thrown from Heaven. If we don't surrender the pride to run our own lives, we will find our eternal resting place not in Heaven but with the enemy.

The second deception the enemy used, caused Eve to doubt God's character, making her believe God was trying to keep something good from her. Again, we can see how many of us fall for the same lie. The fun, entertainment, and pleasure we went looking for ended up being the very things that imprisoned us. God was never trying to keep anything good from us; He was only trying to protect us from certain destruction. After these deceptive tricks, the enemy used one of the most crippling and debilitating lies against Eve. After she had sinned and fallen for his temptation, he condemned her. Condemnation is still the enemy's tool. First, he tricks us into a lifestyle of sin, and then he uses condemnation and shame to keep us from coming to God and finding forgiveness.

God desires us to be right with Him, forgiven and free; if we stop running from Him and start running to Him, we will be free. If you desire more information on this topic, you will find that I give a much more detailed account in my book "Created, Designed by God." Nonetheless, we need to recognize how the enemy attacks so we don't fall prey. The enemy wants to keep us from God because he knows God is the only One who can free us. They say misery loves company, and the devil is determined not to be alone in Hell. So don't let him have your company; run to God, turn your desires over to Him, give Him your life, and let Him transform and change you.

DAY 15
BELIEVE OR BELIEVE

> *Romans 10:9-10*
>
> *"⁹ If you declare with your mouth, "Jesus is Lord," and believe in your heart that God raised Him from the dead, you will be saved. ¹⁰ For it is with your heart that you believe and are justified, and it is with your mouth that you profess your faith and are saved."*

Jesus said in John 3:3, "Very truly I tell you, no one can see the Kingdom of God unless they are born again." If we are not born again, not only can we not enter Heaven, but we can't have the abundant and victorious life God declared. With all that we have been reading and studying, we should have a good understanding of our inability to change without His Divine intervention. Prayerfully, you have decided that God has all the help you need to be successful, and you've grasped your need to be born again, saved, and transformed.

Our passage today explains Salvation. It states that if we declare with our mouths that Jesus is Lord and believe in our hearts that God raised Him from the dead, we will be saved. Through the years, I have met many people who have professed that Jesus is Lord. They "believe" that Jesus is God's son, that He died on the cross, and that He rose again. Regardless of what they say or profess to "believe," they do not live transformed lives. They are still bound by sin, controlled by the flesh nature, and their lives are in shambles. We know that God does not lie. In fact, He cannot lie. It isn't in His character. Therefore, we need to clearly understand what the passage is saying. Our culture has grown accustomed to people saying one thing and doing another. It has become common for people to say what they know others want to hear, never having any intentions of following through. It has gotten so bad that when someone says they will do something, we doubt it to be true and will even ask them to promise. In Biblical times, the disconnect between what one said and did was not nearly as great. In fact, we are instructed in Matthew 5:37 that "All you need to say is simply 'Yes' or 'No'; anything beyond this comes from the evil one." We should be men and women of our word. What we say, we should do. We should never have to swear or promise for people to believe what we are saying is true.

The same is true for what one believes. When someone believes anything, their actions should show it. For example, I believe that the plane I got on to fly overseas could take off, fly, and land safely. My actions proved my beliefs. Since I believed, I purchased a ticket, packed my bags, got a ride to the airport, navigated security, and boarded the plane. If I said I believed that the plane could fly safely but refused to buy a ticket or board a plane, the lack of my actions would prove my disbelief, no matter what I said. I may have all the head knowledge on how planes work. I could even have enough knowledge to build one. Yet, if I refused to board a plane and fly, my actions do not validate my belief. Ultimately, regardless of how much I say that I feel planes are safe, my actions reflect I don't believe it.

The same is true when it comes to our passage today. If we proclaim Jesus is Lord and say we believe God raised Jesus from the dead, then our lives should show it. If we say Jesus is Lord, we are saying He is our Master. A lord rules over; they are the master, and those who are his subjects are his servants. To say Jesus is Lord means we submit to Him and that since He is our Master, He decides what we do and how we live. Proclaiming we believe God raised Jesus from the dead means the penalty of our sin has been paid, and we are free. To say we believe means our life should proclaim that belief. We should live free, forgiven, and empowered to be who He created us to be.

Changed

Day 15 Exercises

1. How have your actions proved you don't fully believe?

2. How do you expect a true believer to live?

3. What does is mean for Jesus to be Lord?

4. What will you be free from once born again and are surrendered completely to His will?

DAY 16
CHILDREN OF GOD

> *John 1:12-13*
>
> *"¹² Yet to all who did receive Him, to those who believed in His name, He gave the right to become children of God ¹³ children born not of natural descent, nor of human decision or a husband's will, but born of God."*

Belief is more than just knowledge of factual events; it is conforming our lives to what we profess to believe. Today's passage says, "To all who did receive Him, to those who believed in His name." The entire point is that we must receive Christ. For clarity, this means we accept Him as our Lord and Savior. Receiving Him is to be saved, transformed, and born again. In Revelation 3:20, it states, "Here I am! I stand at the door and knock. If anyone hears My voice and opens the door, I will come in and eat with that person, and they with Me." To receive Christ is to open the door of our hearts and allow Him to come in and fellowship with us. This fellowship is what sustains us and is what helps us grow in our relationship with Him. For those who may be confused, no, there is not an actual door on your heart; Jesus is not there physically knocking on your heart, and Jesus does not physically move in. This is all a Spiritual occurrence. God's presence and Spirit prompt you with conviction and repentance; this is the knocking. When you answer the Spirit's conviction and His prompting and you repent, that is to open the door of your heart and receive Him. Once you welcome Him, His presence resides in you. His presence in you prompts, guides, and corrects you, always leading you to a stronger relationship with the Lord.

Again, our passage states that "all who receive Him and believe in His name" are given the right to be children of God. The term "right" is important here. A right is something that cannot be taken away or lost. It belongs to you; the only way to lose it is not to accept it or to reject it. A right is very different from a privilege, as privileges are earned and not guaranteed. A right is not earned; it is based on who you are or the nation you belong to. Rights have legal standings and are enforceable. If another violates a right, there are consequences. God's Word declares that all of us who are born again have the right to be "children of God." Once born again, our old identity is gone, and we are now part of God's Kingdom, His chosen people, His elect. The right we have because of who we now are is the right to be His child, and to receive an inheritance from God Himself.

Not only do we have a right to be a child of God, but as His children, we have specific rights and privileges. As His, we have the right to security. We do not have to fear losing our relationship with God. We are not His employees. We are adopted into His family and accepted as His own. This gives us the right of authority. As His, we have authority over sin, the flesh nature, and the enemy. We have the right to intimacy; we are not on the outside looking in, but we can call Him Daddy. This is the intimate type of relationship that is available to all who receive and believe in Him. Finally, we have the right of inheritance; everything that belongs to God has been made available to us. What is in store for us is greater than anything we could ever imagine. With the right of being his child, God has the right of discipline, and God disciplines those He loves. This discipline guides us to all the greatness He has reserved for us. His discipline corrects, guides, and directs us. His discipline is a blessing, not a curse. There are so many more rights given to us as children of God, but the greatest of them all is the identity of being made in His likeness, possessing His character, and being set free from the penalty of our sins. As our passage declares, this transformation is not based on human will but on God's will. Remember, He chooses you. He desires to forgive you and set you free. He wants to come in and commune with you and call you His own.

Changed

Day 16 Exercises

1. Explain the difference between a right and a privilege.

2. What must you do to obtain the right to be a child of God?

3. What would currently change in your life by becoming a child of God?

4. What is standing in the way of you being the child that God has called you to be?

DAY 17

FORGIVEN & FORGOTTEN

> *Hebrews 8:12*
>
> *"And I will forgive their wickedness, and I will never again remember their sins."*

One of our biggest mistakes is attributing finite human qualities to God. He is not confined by human limitations, and He can do that which we cannot. Addressing our passage today, God is able to do something that very few, if any of us, can. He can remember no more. Today's Scripture says that God will forgive our wickedness and never remember our sins. This isn't because God is forgetful or has too much on His mind. No, this is because once we receive Christ, we are no longer the same old person. Christ paid the penalty that was due for our wickedness. Once the debt is paid, the debt is not held over our heads. This is how God can and does choose to remember our sins no more. The penalty has been satisfied, the account wiped clean, and we are set free.

Suppose you could imagine owing an impossible debt to pay, not fifty or a hundred dollars, but a hundred billion dollars. This is the kind of debt that none of us, no matter what we do, would ever be able to satisfy. We could work every day of our lives and never have an impact on such a debt. This is, unfortunately, what our sin is like to God. No matter how good we try to be, no matter how much we volunteer, or even how much we give to others, our sin still requires a payment that is impossible for us to satisfy. One of the most famous and quoted Bible verses is John 3:16: "For this is how God loved the world: He gave His one and only Son so that everyone who believes in Him will not perish but have eternal life." His love for us and His desire to set us free caused Him to make a way for our debt to be paid.

We need to realize that God did all the work necessary. Our sins can be remembered no more, and our wickedness is forgiven without us having to make it right or fix it. All we have to do is accept the gift given to us in and through Jesus. The enemy would have us believe that being in a right relationship with God is impossible and that God can't forgive us for all we have done. He uses condemnation and shame to make us hide from God. He knows that as long as we are held in bondage by our past mistakes, we will never surrender to the Lord and find freedom.

There was a time in my life when I fell for this condemnation and felt God could not use me because of my shame and guilt. I knew God had called me to serve Him, but I had been living to please myself and not Him. This led me to lustful thinking, a lifestyle of seeking pleasures, and eventually addicted to tobacco and alcohol. The more I partook of these fleshly pleasures, the more I felt dirty and the less I thought God could ever use me. The worst part is there were times I tried to clean myself up and would take what I deemed to be the necessary steps to be right with God. All of these self-imposed attempts at righteousness only left me feeling worse. Since I was trying to accomplish holiness in my own power, I failed every time. I was only giving the enemy more and more to condemn me with. I always ended up feeling worse than when I started.

When I finally realized that Jesus had done all the work necessary for my freedom and all I had to do was accept it, I finally experienced freedom. I went from having a regimented religious experience to having a relationship. In a relationship with God, I was delivered from my past and set free from my condemnation. I finally realized, if God remembered my sins no more, then I should not hold them against myself either.

Changed

Day 17 Exercises

1. What are some of the things you have felt condemnation or shame over?

_____
_____
_____
_____
_____
_____
_____
_____

2. Describe the difference between religion and relationship?

_____
_____
_____
_____
_____
_____
_____
_____

3. What has prevented you from accepting God's forgiveness?

_____
_____
_____
_____
_____
_____
_____
_____

4. What impact does it have on you to know that God will remember your sins no more?

_____
_____
_____
_____
_____
_____
_____
_____

DAY 18

HEALED & CHANGED

> *1 Peter 2:24*
>
> *"He himself bore our sins" in His body on the cross, so that we might die to sins and live for righteousness; "by His wounds you have been healed."*

Change is hard. The first reason is that we don't really want to change. We say we do and might even want to be free from the inevitable consequences, but we aren't looking for a total transformation. If you feel argumentative, take a moment to examine all the times you desperately wanted change. Now, determine if you were sick and tired of living to please yourself and doing things your way, or were you tired of the results that came from selfish living. There is a big difference between wanting change and wanting the effects changed. Beyond not designing genuine change, we have been Spiritually blind to what God has already accomplished for us. We must get real about our motives and desires. If we are not honest with ourselves, we will never be able to surrender to God and find healing. Almost 2,000 years ago, Jesus paid the penalty for our sins so we could be free. Our passage today clearly says Jesus paid the price so that we can live for righteousness.

In John chapter 5, there is the story of a man who was born lame and remained lame for 38 years. This man seemed desperate for change. His situation warranted change, and there seems to be no question about his desire to change his condition. Reading about the lame man and his encounter with Jesus, we find him lying at a pool called Bethesda, hoping to be healed. This pool was a gathering place for those lame, blind, or sick. It was believed that when the waters of the pool were stirred, the first person to enter the pool would be healed. I don't know if people were ever healed by entering the waters or if everyone who got in after the waters moved just assumed someone made it in before them. When Jesus meets this man, He asks him a very straightforward question in verse 6 of John chapter 5: "Do you want to get well?". This seems like a silly question to ask as the man obviously desired to walk. Yet, Jesus asks Him anyway. We can learn something from this in our own lives. The truth is no matter how much it seems we should obviously desire to change, we have to answer the question Jesus asked, "Do you want to get well?" The way the lame man answered is how most of us answer Jesus, too.

The man responds to Jesus in verse 7 with "Sir, I have no one to help me into the pool when the water is stirred. While I am trying to get in, someone else goes down ahead of me." The man's response was to list all the reasons why he couldn't be healed. His first response is to blame others for not helping him. Then, to top it all off, he makes excuses as to why he can't do it for himself. It seems he even resigns to the fact that others have been able to be changed, but there is no way he can. All of this describes each of us. God is not concerned with our limitations, the blame we place on others, or even the self-pity which holds us back. The Lord is not limited by any of the things which limit us. He simply wants us to tell Him we are ready to be healed. The way Jesus responds to this man is how He responds to us. He told the man to "Get up! Pick up your mat and walk," and the man got up and walked. The lame man was changed. He was healed. No magic words were needed, no stirring of the pool or even a bright light. All the man had to do was receive and believe the words of Christ, and he was healed. Before you start making the excuse that it was different for him because Jesus was there, our passage today states that "by His wounds, we are healed." (Isaiah 53:5) This means our change is complete. It is indisputable. All we have to do is receive, believe, and act on it. Then, just like the lame man, we can get up changed, healed, and whole.

Changed

Day 18 Exercises

1. Do you want to be changed? Why?

___

2. What excuses or reason have you given that have prevented you from changing?

___

3. Share about those who have been successful in changing and how they did it.

___

4. What more must God do for you to be changed?

___

DAY 19
LIVING IT UP

> *Titus 2:11-12*
>
> *"*[11] *For the grace of God has appeared that offers salvation to all people.* [12] *It teaches us to say "No" to ungodliness and worldly passions, and to live self-controlled, upright and godly lives in this present age."*

We have seen that God has already done everything necessary for our freedom. We have addressed the lie of condemnation and should have reached a point in our understanding that when we come to God sincerely in repentance, He forgives us and no longer holds our past against us. Today's passage reaffirms that He offers Salvation to all people. This includes us, regardless of where we were born, our nationality, or even our crimes against God. We are His creation, and just like any loving parent, He longs for our relationship with Him to be restored and renewed.

The passage today even takes it a step beyond Salvation and states His grace, the same grace that calls us to be His, also teaches us how to live. Please pay attention as verse 12 states that we are taught to say "no to ungodliness and worldly passions." This is important as many people wrongly assume temptation will be removed upon Salvation. They think their flesh nature will never raise its ugly head and try to lead them to sin. The truth is, we must be the ones to say no. His grace will teach us how, His Spirit will change our desires, but the flesh will still cry out for control. The difference after Salvation is that as we are His; we have a power greater than ourselves which enables us to say no. Before our transformation, the flesh nature controlled us. Our genetics, both physical and Spiritual, and all those other influences that made us who we were are what dictated our fleshly desires. After being born again, our transformation in and through Christ becomes what impacts our desires and enables us to say no to the flesh. Even so, we must be the ones to say no; God's Spirit will empower us, but we still have to do it.

There is no magical moment that our flesh will never cry out to be fed. However, according to 1 Corinthians 10, after receiving and believing in Christ, there is no temptation we will face that God won't provide a way out of, and there are no natural desires that His presence in us can't overcome. Even better, once transformed, we cannot only say no to the flesh, but we can also live "self-controlled and upright lives." This is not a possibility or a suggestion but rather, a cause and effect. If you cannot say no to those worldly desires, then either you have not been born again or you have not been saying no to the flesh.

I once heard an illustration of two dogs on a porch: a bad dog and a good dog. The question is posed: if they fight, who will win? The answer is the one you feed the most. This is true for us as well. If we are not saying no to the flesh nature, then we are feeding the bad dog. The more we feed it, the stronger it is. The stronger it is, the harder it is to say no, and we end up feeding it more. It gets stronger and stronger, and God's Spirit within us becomes easier and easier to ignore. Before you know it, we can't hear God at all. Now, this illustration is just to help you understand. Please know that regardless of how much we feed the flesh, it will never be stronger than God and will never be able to defeat His Spirit. God is above all and will always be able to overcome. When we feed the flesh nature more than the Spirit, we become deaf to God's voice and blind to His guidance, and in that condition, our ability to say no to "ungodliness and worldly passions" is severely hindered.

Changed

Day 19 Exercises

1. List ways you have been feeding the flesh nature.

_____
_____
_____
_____
_____
_____
_____

2. List ways you can feed the Spirit.

_____
_____
_____
_____
_____
_____
_____
_____

3. What does an upright life looks like?

_____
_____
_____
_____
_____
_____
_____
_____

4. What does it mean to you when you read in the passage that He empowers us to say no?

_____
_____
_____
_____
_____
_____
_____
_____

DAY 20
UNDER ATTACK

> *1 Peter 5:8*
>
> *"Be alert and of sober mind. Your enemy the devil prowls around like a roaring lion looking for someone to devour.."*

The first thing we must come to grips with concerning our freedom and the passage today is that the devil is not a metaphor for sinful or evil thoughts and desires. The devil is a real being who is our enemy and, according to John 10:10, only wants to "steal, kill, and destroy." Today's Scripture specifies that we must be "alert and of sober mind." Being sober-minded means being serious, focused, and ready. Many of us know that when substances are used, and we lose our sobriety, our thinking is often misguided, and our judgments are off. At those times, we are most vulnerable to the enemy's attack. I want to point out that we can abstain from substance use and still be lost in our thinking with the desires of the flesh and the pride of life.

The greatest trick of any enemy is to make us believe there is no enemy and that he doesn't exist. If we do not believe that any nation wants to harm or control us, we will conclude that since we have no enemies, there is no need to train military personnel or produce and have offensive and defensive weapons. Can you imagine what shape America would be in if we had no military presence, no Army, Navy, Air Force, Marines, or Coast Guard? How long would it be before we realized we have enemies who want to possess and control our nation, people, and resources?

The same is true for us Spiritually. If the devil can make us believe he is not real and we don't need to worry about him, we will not be prepared to overcome him. The Bible is clear. We are in Spiritual warfare. In fact, Ephesians chapter 6, verses 10-17, tells us how to prepare for this battle. "Finally, be strong in the Lord and in His mighty power. Put on the full armor of God so that you can take your stand against the devil's schemes. For our struggle is not against flesh and blood, but against the rulers, against the authorities, against the powers of this dark world, and against the spiritual forces of evil in the Heavenly realms. Therefore, put on the full armor of God so that when the day of evil comes, you may be able to stand your ground and, after you have done everything, to stand. Stand firm then, with the belt of truth buckled around your waist, with the breastplate of righteousness in place, and with your feet fitted with the readiness that comes from the Gospel of peace. In addition to all this, take up the shield of faith, with which you can extinguish all the flaming arrows of the evil one. Take the helmet of salvation and the sword of the Spirit, which is the word of God."

If there were not an enemy, there would not be a battle, and there would be no need for God's armor. Recognize that there is an enemy lurking in the shadows, waiting for you to drop your guard, forget your armor, or be caught up serving the flesh. It is only then that he can mount a successful attack on you. However, the enemy will never be able to overcome you when you are ready, prepared, and clothed in God's armor. Simply feed the Spirit (feed yourself with the things of God) and not the flesh (don't feed worldly pleasures, lust, or pride), and you will stand upright, alert, and sober, and with His help, you will always overcome the enemy's attack.

Changed

Day 20 Exercises

1. Explain what you know about the enemy.

_____
_____
_____
_____
_____
_____
_____
_____

2. What does being alert and sober mean to you?

_____
_____
_____
_____
_____
_____
_____
_____

3. How should you prepare for a daily battle against the enemy? Be specific and explain.

_____
_____
_____
_____
_____
_____
_____
_____

4. How do you get God's Spirit in you? List ways you can feed His Spirit.

_____
_____
_____
_____
_____
_____
_____
_____

DAY 21
SEALED & DELIVERED

> *Ephesians 1:13*
>
> *"And you also were included in Christ when you heard the message of truth, the Gospel of your salvation. When you believed, you were marked in him with a seal, the promised Holy Spirit,"*

Today, we see the word "believed" in our passage. We should already fully understand this is more than knowledge. To believe is to live out what you declare in your everyday life, both in speech and deed. As discussed before, once we receive Christ and believe, we are marked and sealed with the "promised Holy Spirit." When this passage was written in Roman times, it was common to use a seal as an identifying mark to show possession. These seals were often placed on contracts, letters, or documents to validate authenticity. So when we read we are marked with a seal in Christ, it is to identify we are His and belong to Him.

Not only are we sealed with His mark, but the seal is the Holy Spirit Himself. The Holy Spirit is the third person of the Trinity. The Trinity is God the Father, God the Son, and God the Holy Spirit. These three equal persons are entirely God. They are not three separate gods but the One and Only God. The Trinity is hard to comprehend as we are limited in our knowledge, but the Bible clearly teaches that there is only One God, yet when we go to the beginning and look at creation, God said, "Let Us make man in Our Image." (Genesis 1:26) Then, in the New Testament, Jesus stated, "Anyone who has seen Me has seen the Father." (John 14:9) Even if we can't fully understand how the three are One yet separate and equal, we can have confidence that we are sealed with the Holy Spirit, which is God, upon being born again.

We must understand that God didn't just set things into motion and then leave and return to Heaven. He is not distant. In fact, He is the exact opposite of distant. God is so involved, so present, and cares so much for us. Once we are born again, He places Himself, in the form of the Holy Spirit, in us. His Spirt not only guides us but is our counselor, comforter, and friend. This means that what we face in life, we don't face alone. We just talked about having an enemy that tries to attack us. One of the tactics he often uses to attack us is to make us feel alone. This is a lie; God has declared in His Word that He will never leave us nor forsake us. (Hebrews 13:5) This means we will never be alone; regardless of how alone we may feel, He is always there.

Being sealed with the Holy Spirit, knowing I am never alone but that He is always with me, has allowed me to face the things life throws my way much differently. Instead of being overwhelmed, fearful, and defeated, I now rest in the assurance that the One who created me, the One who designed me, and the One who loves me more than I love myself will see me through. I sometimes have to remind myself God doesn't always calm the storm. Sometimes, He takes us through it. This is the confidence that I now possess. Anytime doubt or frustration may try to come; I remind myself the same God that split the Red Sea, protected His children in the fire, and raised the dead is the same God that resides in me. If I had any doubt regarding His power moving in and through me on my behalf, Ephesians chapter 1 tells us that the same power that raised Christ from the dead and seated Him at the right hand of the Father is the same power that lives in all who believe. You are sealed with His power and authority if you are His. What can't you do through Him?

Changed

Day 21 Exercises

1. What does your life say you believe?

2. How does being sealed with the Holy Spirit make you feel?

3. What does it mean to you to know that the same power that raised Christ from the dead resides in you?

4. Explain why you don't currently live in the power and authority that you should since God lives in you.

Week 4

> *"We are not physical beings having a Spiritual experience, we are Spiritual beings having a physical experience."*

Grasping that we are not seeking a spiritual enlightening, spiritual revelation, or any other type of momentarily spiritual experience, but that we are already spiritual beings having a momentary physical experience is essential. So many people are living like this is all there is, that one day they will die, and it will all be over. This simply is not true. We all will continue to exist for eternity. We are not simply flesh and blood; we have an immaterial and eternal soul. This soul will continue to exist long after we have taken our last breath. Our life here on earth will determine where we will spend eternity. This is not based on good works but simply on if you have surrendered to Christ and have accepted Him as Lord and Savior.

We talk so much about finding eternal life, accepting Jesus as your Savior, being born again, and living in Heaven forever. Many have come to believe if you aren't saved, you die, and that is it; there is nothing more. That is an incorrect interpretation. While it's true those born again will receive eternal life, the assumption that those who do not believe will simply miss out on an eternal existence is incorrect. The truth is, we will all live forever. To give a simple explanation, if we are saved, we will live forever in a relationship with God in an eternal paradise. If we are not saved, we will live eternally separated from God's presence in a place of eternal torment. Since we are eternal spiritual beings, what we are experiencing here on earth is only a fleeting moment.

Knowing this should propel us to live a life that focuses on what is truly important. Instead of spending all our time and resources living for the here and now, we should be investing in our future and investing our time and resources in the hereafter. If you stop and examine your life at this moment, you will probably see that you have been prioritizing the wrong aspects of your life. You will likely find you have worked hard to meet your physical needs for food and shelter. You may even find that much of your energy, efforts, and resources have gone into fulfilling fleshly desires like fun, entertainment, substances, relationships, and material possessions. This is backward. All these things will be used up, and eventually gone, yet we generally make them the most important.

Instead, we should seek to feed our souls by growing in our relationship with God. The Bible clearly tells us not to worry about all the temporary stuff. Matthew 6:33 states, "But seek first His Kingdom and His righteousness, and all these things will be given to you as well." God knows what we need better than we do. He knows what is right for us and what will benefit us. We need to trust Him. If we spend this life seeking Him, honoring Him, and serving Him, we will find the abundant life He promised us not only in the hereafter but also in the here and now. In the 12 steps, we are told to take a fearless and searching inventory of our lives. In this inventory, not only should we look at what we have done and the impact of those actions, but we should also search ourselves and see how we have made the less important into the most important.

This is a good time to look beyond our actions and look for patterns in our families, finding patterns of physical abuse, substance use, unhealthy relationships, materialism, and other behaviors. Many of these behaviors, as well as specific physical and emotional conditions, could be signs of generational sins. These generational sins are a Spiritual problem and must be dealt with in prayer and broken by the Spirit of God. We often try to fix things that are out of the scope of our abilities, and when we fail, we give up and stop trying. When dealing with generational issues, we need not give up, but give in to the Lord and allow Him to bring deliverance and healing.

Don't forget to look at past and current relationships. Close relationships, sexual or not, create soul ties. Paul writes in 1 Corinthians 6:16, "Do you not know that he who unites himself with a prostitute is one with her in body? For it is said, the two will become one flesh." This verse explains participation in a strictly physical relationship with no emotional ties creates a union between two people. It further explains that this union takes the two and makes them one. When we consider a purely physical encounter creates a union, or soul tie, with the other individual, how much more so are soul ties created when our emotional being unites with the emotional being of another? This is the union of two souls. We need God to bring back all we have given away to others that doesn't belong to them, and we need God to sever all the ties we are dragging along in our lives that do not belong.

As you are searching your life and preparing to surrender all these areas to God, don't overlook the effects of negative expectations. We become what we believe ourselves to be. Psychologists teach people that they can't live in a way they do not view themselves to be. Plainly put, if I believe I will fail, then I will fail. If I believe I can't change, I won't be able to. If I am confident I can't live a Christ-like life, I won't. On the contrary, if I believe God's Word is true and that He can work in and through me so that I can live a righteous and holy life, then I will allow God to do so, and I will live a life worthy of my calling as a child of God.

Choosing to see ourselves as God does is key to living in victory. We are not trapped by our past or the past of our family. We are designed and defined by God. You can read more about all of this in my book "Created, Designed by God." As we begin our fourth week together, be committed to accepting all God says about you and to you by faith. He is the One who created you, and He is the One who can fix anything awry in your life. Reject the enemy's lies and know that you are not the sum of your mistakes.

DAY 22
BITTERNESS

> *Hebrews 12:15*
>
> *"See to it that no one falls short of the grace of God and that no bitter root grows up to cause trouble and defile many."*

In my years of ministry, I have met many people who have endured awful things, like physical, sexual, and mental abuse, traumatic events, and even the complete absence of loving parental figures. Our society has made it acceptable for those wronged to be bitter, jaded, and angry. These individuals often use their experiences as reasons for their lives being a mess. Society tends to make excuses for their bad behavior and often co-signs on these individuals' right to be bitter and angry. The problem is, unless they take personal responsibility for their own decisions, they will never recognize they have the ability to do what is necessary to be free. As long as they blame the abuse, the abusers, and the trauma they have experienced, they will never find healing and freedom in Christ.

Our passage today clarifies that bitterness will destroy us. I once read a sign that stated: "Being bitter is like drinking cyanide and wishing the other person to die." Bitterness causes us to be forever stuck as a victim. Choosing bitterness, revenge, anger, or unforgiveness makes us a continual victim of the original offenses, as well as a victim to the consequences of a bitter life. Many right now are thinking, if you had been through what I have, you would understand and be bitter, too. My goal is not to make light of anyone's pain or shift the blame from the perpetrator to the victim. It is my goal to help you see that victory and healing can be yours if you choose it. Many people have overcome abuse equal to if not worse than, what you may have endured and have gone on to live very successful lives. The difference between those who overcome and those who are stuck is that overcomers simply choose to no longer be the victim but to be victorious. In order to be victorious, they had to choose to release their bitterness. They didn't make this choice because their abuser deserved it. They chose to release bitterness because they deserved to be free from the hatred that had destroyed them.

I have avoided saying the next step in releasing bitterness because I know that for many, the next step seems impossible, but the next step is absolutely necessary if we are going to find the life God has in store for us. The next step in releasing bitterness is forgiveness. Again, we do not necessarily forgive because the person deserves it but because we deserve it. The Bible is clear on the need for forgiveness. Jesus Himself said in Matthew 6:14-15, "For if you forgive other people when they sin against you, your Heavenly Father will also forgive you. But if you do not forgive others their sins, your Father will not forgive your sins." The principle of your release being tied to the release you give others is clearly taught. Other Scriptures say, "Give, and it will be given to you" (Luke 6:38), "sow generously and receive generously" (2 Corinthians 9:6), and "whatever a man sows that he will reap" (Galatians 6:9). Christ set the example for us; He was beaten, mocked, spat on, hair ripped out, humiliated, and nailed to a cross for no crime whatsoever. He did nothing to deserve what happened to Him. He could have stopped it but chose not to so that He could fulfill God's plan for mankind. Amidst it all, He said, "Father, forgive them, for they know not what they do" (Luke 23:24). He chose forgiveness. We, too, should choose forgiveness. He chose it so that God's plan could be fulfilled in and through Him, and we, too, should choose forgiveness so that God's plan can be fulfilled in and through us. Search your life and see where you have allowed bitterness to cripple you. Then choose to let go of that bitterness by coming to God for healing. In doing so, you will be choosing to no longer be the victim but to be victor.

Changed

Day 22 Exercises

1. What have you felt justified in being bitter about?

2. How has being bitter hurt you?

3. How do you feel about this statement: forgiveness does not mean you have to submit to further abuse or even befriend the one you are forgiving?

4. Share what you are doing to release bitterness in your life.

DAY 23
CHECK YOURSELF

> *2 Corinthians 13:5*
>
> *"Examine yourselves to see whether you are in the faith; test yourselves. Do you not realize that Christ Jesus is in you unless, of course, you fail the test?"*

The Scripture today states to "examine yourself" to make sure that you are "in the faith." Following this passage is key to the change we desire. There are way too many people who identify as Christian but are not in the faith. They know in their minds who Jesus is, they deem the Bible true, and they may even be actively involved in religious activities, but they are not in the faith. They think they are, but on the day they meet Christ face to face, they will hear Jesus say, "I never knew you. Get away from me, you who break God's laws (Matthew 7:23).

Thinking you are right and being wrong is a terrible place to be. It is better to know you need to change than to go through life believing you are right with God only to find out on Judgment Day that you are not. Revelation 3:15-16 reads, "I know your deeds, that you are neither cold nor hot. I wish you were either one or the other! So, because you are lukewarm—neither hot nor cold—I am about to spit you out of my mouth." Too many so-called believers are simply living in a perpetual lukewarm state. God will not honor a lukewarm life. His expectation is for us to be completely in, as Revelation 3 puts it, to be hot. Understand that He does not desire us to live a cold life, a life that is distant from Him, or a life which desperately needs change. He does, however, desire for us to be one or the other because at least if we are cold, we know we need to change, and we are open to His help.

Today's passage is asking us to examine our lives and see if we are proving a "hot" life for Christ or if our lives fall within the "lukewarm" or "cold" spectrum. Understand today's passage is clear, if Christ is really living in us, we will pass the faith test, and our lives will show it. If we do not know Him or only have factual knowledge of Him, our lives will also verify our lack of faith. Without getting back into the difference between believing and having knowledge, I want to lay some groundwork for a faith test. What does a tested and true faith look like? If we look to Scripture, it clearly describes a believer as one who will hear the Lord say, "Well done, my good and faithful servant," looks like (Matthew 25:21). We must remember that there is no in-between. You will either hear "well done" or "depart from me." In order to pass the faith test, our lives must have a distinct testimony that verifies our professed beliefs. The Scriptures state: "If you love Me, you will obey Me," and "By this everyone will know that you are my disciples if you love one another" (John 14:15 NLT and John 13:35 NIV). Our obedience to God's Word and our love for mankind is our distinct testimony. Sincere worship is another test of our faith. True worship is to give everything to God: our lives, money, and time. Another way to examine your faith is to see if your life displays the fruit of the Spirit.

The fruit of the Spirit is the visible, identifiable evidence of a life that belongs to Christ. Galatians 5:22-23 states: "But the fruit of the Spirit is love, joy, peace, forbearance, kindness, goodness, faithfulness, gentleness and self-control. Against such things, there is no law." There must be clear, indisputable evidence in our lives that we belong to Him if we are going to pass the testing of our faith. While none of us are perfect and each of us may fall short in some if not all of these areas, a true believer will show growth in all the above. If and when they miss the mark, true conviction and repentance will come.

Changed

Day 23 Exercises

1. Share how your attitudes and behaviors exhibit or fail to exhibit the fruit of the Spirit.

___

2. What do you spend the majority of your time doing?

___

3. How does your life bear witness that you are hot, cold, or luke-warm?

___

4. What do you need to surrender to God in order to hear "well done my good and faithful servant?"

___

DAY 24
DEEP INSIDE

> *Lamentations 3:40*
>
> *"Let us examine our ways and test them, and let us return to the Lord."*

Examining our ways and testing our faith is critical to ensuring we are right with God. A right relationship with God is the only way we will make beneficial and lasting changes. Understanding how our actions and behaviors affect others helps us not fall back into our old ways. Getting real with the hurt, destruction, and disappointment our behaviors and lifestyles have caused is essential. This includes the effects of substance use, but in reality, selfishness, pride, and materialism also profoundly impact those around us. When examining your ways, don't overlook those blaring lifestyle problems, but also don't ignore areas that may be socially acceptable, yet clearly out of God's design for us. Those "acceptable" sins are just as devastating regardless of the majority view or popularity.

Today, we want to examine if we are living out what we claim to believe and the impact not living by God's Word has had on our lives. Ultimately, we want to know how we have hurt others and how much our sin has broken God's heart. This will require us to list names or situations where we have wronged others. I want to encourage you not to limit your time on this to one day as we navigate to the end of this process. We should continue to address the wrongs we've committed as God brings them to remembrance. We need to develop a lifestyle of repentance; it is not a one-time thing but an everyday choice. When God reveals an area where we have sinned against Him and wronged another or ourselves, we must repent. Again, repentance means to turn from that which we are repenting of. Repentance is more than just being sorry or sorry we got caught. It is genuine sorrow for the hurt we have caused God, others, and ourselves.

When Godly sorrow is experienced, we will turn from that which has hindered our relationship with Him and do what is necessary to be Holy as the Bible says, "Be Holy because I am Holy." (1 Peter 1:16). Holiness is the standard. It is not a suggestion, but it is an expectation. Accomplishing this on our own is impossible, but by surrendering to Christ, being born again, and allowing Him to live in and through us we can all be Holy. Holiness is not something we have to figure out, work at, or even strive to achieve. Holiness is simply surrendering to His Spirit within us and being obedient to His will.

In my life, I have struggled with many things. A few of these struggles were with fleshly desires, materialism, and alcohol. There have been many more, but these three areas were personal struggles that I felt didn't affect anybody but myself. Believing these areas only affected me, I actually felt no need to change. My thought process was that it was my money and time. I didn't think my actions were hurting anyone. The truth is, I didn't want to change. I enjoyed what I was doing and was having fun doing it. The worst part is I thought I was saved since I had a head knowledge of Jesus. One day, God woke me up. He revealed what I thought wasn't hurting anybody had destroyed my life and my relationship with my family. I was living paycheck to paycheck and had nothing to show for it but a bunch of stuff I didn't need and couldn't afford. What was once a weekend party had now become a necessity. It was only when I lost all hope that God revealed how my sins had ruined my life and the lives of those around me. God then showed me how much my disobedience hurt Him and how much He loves me. It was then I knew I needed a change that only God could bring. I repented, and He forgave me. That was instantaneous, but becoming mature enough to live out my faith was a process. The Good News for me and you is that we don't have to navigate that process alone; He is there with us to help us each step of the way.

Changed

Day 24 Exercises

1. Make a list of all the sinful choices you have made that you thought only impacted you, but now realize hurt all those around you.

_____
_____
_____
_____
_____
_____
_____
_____
_____

2. What is the biggest regret I carry?

_____
_____
_____
_____
_____
_____
_____
_____
_____

3. In what ways have I broken God's heart?

_____
_____
_____
_____
_____
_____
_____
_____

4. List the names of people that your sinful choices impacted and how it affected them

_____
_____
_____
_____
_____
_____
_____
_____

DAY 25
COMPARING

> *Galatians 6:4*
>
> *"Each one should test their own actions. Then they can take pride in themselves alone, without comparing themselves to someone else."*

People like to compare. We shouldn't, but we do. We compare everything: jobs, houses, cars, kids, and even spouses. Sometimes, comparing motivates us to be better, try harder, and do more. Other times, comparing has the opposite effect. It discourages and cripples individuals, making them think they will never measure up. Comparing can drive us to "keep up with the Joneses." We see what they have and want the same thing or something bigger or better. The jealousy associated with comparing drives us to purchase things we can't afford or don't even need. This brings on a massive debt that forces us to work more hours to pay for unnecessary things. All of this wastes the time we could be building our relationship with God, our families, and our friends, leaving us financially, spiritually, and emotionally bankrupt.

First Timothy 6:6 says, "Godliness with contentment is great gain." When we learn to be content with a relationship with God, we will stop comparing and be able to apply today's passage to test our own actions. Notice I said content with a relationship with God, not content in our relationship with God. We should always desire to have a better and deeper relationship with the Lord. The contentment we are to have is in knowing everything in life flows from our relationship with Him. Matthew chapter six tells us to "seek first the Kingdom of God, and these things will be added to you." The Bible is clear that everything we need in life will be given to us through our relationship with God. We need not compare ourselves to others but simply seek God, and we will have the desires of our heart.

How this all works is simple: the more we seek God, the better our relationship with Him will be. The better our relationship is, the more we change. The more we change, the more our desires become His desires. The closer we get to the Lord, the more we want His will for our lives and the less we desire the things of this world. A fruit of the Spirit (evidence of a right relationship with God) is peace. Peace and contentment go hand in hand. When we become content with our relationship with God, we will be at peace and not feel the need to compare ourselves to others.

The second part of all this is to test ourselves. Testing ourselves is the same as examining ourselves, but in our passage today, it specifically means checking our relationship, lifestyle, and heart to ensure we are walking with God in all areas. People often stop growing in their relationship with the Lord because the ones they are following have stopped growing. This is another reason why we are not to be compared to someone else. We are all human, and all fall short of God's Glory. If our standard is set to that of another fallen human being, we will fall even shorter from where we are called to be. The standard of our measure is to be Jesus, not anyone else. Testing and measuring ourselves to the perfection of Christ will keep us humble and cause us to continue to seek the Lord's help in becoming who He created us to be. Our passage today tells us to take pride in this, for drawing closer and closer to the Lord is the only thing that matters. The key to life and the key to victory is only found in Him.

Changed

Day 25 Exercises

1. Who have I compared myself to and why?

2. Do my desires line up with God's Word?

3. How do I fall short when comparing myself to Jesus?

4. What am I proud about in my life, do these areas line up with what God desires?

DAY 26
DISQUALIFIED

> *1 Corinthians 6:9-10*
>
> *"⁹ Or do you not know that the unrighteous will not inherit the Kingdom of God? Do not be deceived; neither the sexually immoral, nor idolaters, nor adulterers, nor homosexuals, ¹⁰ nor thieves, nor the greedy, nor those habitually drunk, nor verbal abusers, nor swindlers, will inherit the Kingdom of God." (NASB)*

The life we live affects more than just ourselves, and our decisions impact others. I have shared with you how I lived in deception, believing I was right with God even though my life didn't show it. I pray that God has opened your eyes to where you currently stand with Him. It would be awful to die believing you belong to Him only to find out you don't. Today's passage gives a list of lifestyles that are in direct conflict with being born again, saved, and transformed. The passage states that anyone living these particular lifestyles "will not inherit the Kingdom of God." The Kingdom it is referring to is Heaven. Heaven is reserved for God's chosen people, His elect, who have believed in and received Jesus Christ as their Lord and Savior. Those who have rejected the call or only went through the motions with no change of heart, behavior, or desires will forever be separated from the presence of God in the eternal torment of Hell.

The list of disqualifications holds some unmistakable lifestyles that are at odds with righteousness and Holiness, but it also lists some that might not be so obvious. We must remember cultures change continually. What society deems to be normal, moral, and acceptable is not constant. For example, many years ago, if a woman was caught in adultery, she would be shamed, ostracized, and even made to wear a scarlet letter. Now, it is the cultural norm for both men and women to have multiple partners and live together before marriage. Drinking alcohol once prohibited is now acceptable and heavily advertised. Society may set cultural standards, but they do not set God's standards. Malachi 3:6 states, "For I the Lord do not change," and Hebrews 13:8 says, "Jesus Christ is the same yesterday and today and forever." This means what God has declared unrighteous is still unrighteous, regardless of what is now acceptable or legal.

This being said, I want to speak on God's declared unrighteous acts briefly. God said, "The unrighteous will not inherit the Kingdom of God." He says, "Do not be deceived," This means stop justifying what He declares wrong and stop looking to mankind for approval. God will not find you innocent just because the masses find it okay. God said the sexually immoral will not enter Heaven. Sexual immorality is any sexual activity outside of marriage. This includes pornography, premarital sex, adultery, lust, and more. Idolatry is not just a golden image one bows to or prays to. Idolatry is anything that takes God's rightful place as number one in our lives. This means a job, a relationship, money, material possessions, and even self can be an idol. It goes on to talk about homosexuals, adulterers, thieves, the greedy, drunkards, and swindlers. Some of these are currently acceptable in our society, but God clearly states these lifestyles will disqualify us from the Kingdom. It also states verbal abusers, which include those who insult, humiliate, intimidate, slander, and gossip about others will not inherit the Kingdom.

As you can see, when we examine ourselves, there is no way, without God's help, for us ever to measure up. First Corinthians 6:11 clarifies this by saying, "And that is what some of you were. But you were washed, sanctified, and justified in the name of the Lord Jesus Christ and by the Spirit of our God." The key to this is not what we were. The measure isn't if we used to be stuck in these lifestyles. Rather, the key is if we are still stuck in them.

Changed

Day 26 Exercises

1. What current unrighteous lifestyles do you struggle with?

2. What unrighteous lifestyles have you overcome?

3. Why is it impossible to be right with God and actively participating in unrighteousness?

4. If you surrender the areas you are struggling with to the Lord what will happen?

DAY 27
FALL SHORT

> *Hebrews 4:1*
>
> *"Therefore, since the promise of entering his rest still stands, let us be careful that none of you be found to have fallen short of it."*

Reading our passage today reminds us that God has promised we can enter His rest. The rest it refers to goes beyond the eternal rest from sickness, sadness, and pain we will find in Heaven. The rest we are reading about here also includes the rest we find in the peace that comes from a life of faith in God. This faith is built on all the promises of God that are given throughout the Bible. Promises like: "He will never leave nor forsake us," that "He will work all things together for good," and "if He is for us, nothing can stand against us" (Deut. 31:6, Romans 8:28, 31). He also promises to give us a new nature upon being born again. This new nature will no longer be ruled by the flesh but driven by His Spirit. We could keep talking about His promises forever, but for today, I want to remind you of only one more. We are promised eternal life and an abundant life filled with love, joy, peace, patience, kindness, goodness, faithfulness, gentleness, and self-control.

While this is wonderful, and we can take extreme comfort in the truth of God's promises, this passage reminds us to "be careful" and ensure that we don't fall short of entering His rest and finding His promises. All of God's promises have a qualification that must be met to receive them. Our passage says, "Be careful," so that none of us will be found to "have fallen short." This places the responsibility on us, not God. God has done everything necessary for us to receive His promises, and He has clearly defined the one and only qualifier to receive them. It remains up to us to meet the qualification. The only qualification of God's promises is to be born again. Once born again, all of God's promises become ours. This is beyond His promises just being available to us; they become our right, our inheritance, and should be our expectation. We should walk and live in confidence in all God has declared. The faith and knowledge that God will fulfill His promises in the here and now, as well as the hereafter, should change everything. Since God has promised to forgive us, to remember our sins no more, to transform us, to give us His nature, to change our desires, and to set us free from sin and the effects of sin, there is simply no way for us to live bound and trapped in sin.

We need to understand there are only two reasons we remain powerless to be who He has promised us to be. Once we understand, we will know why we must continually examine ourselves. We need to ensure we are not falling short of entering His rest. The only reason we can be found to have fallen short of entering His rest is that we are not born again. Remember, this is the qualifier. We must be born again to receive His promises, including the promise of His rest. This is where so many are; they simply are not saved. The unsaved fall into many categories: those who deny God, those who know He is real but reject Him, and those who go beyond rejection and choose a blasphemous lifestyle. Then there are those on the opposite side; they know He is real but are waiting for the right time to surrender, or worse, they know He is real, believe He is the way, and even have gone through the motions of surrender but fail to submit fully. Believing we are right with God on an eternal level but failing to grasp that a saved life is a changed life is the worst place to be. There is no way to be born again, transformed, and still be the same old person. This is why we must carefully examine ourselves and ensure we don't fall short. The only other reason a born again believer may struggle is they simply don't know or believe that God's promises are for them.

Changed

Day 27 Exercises

1. Where do you feel you may be falling short of entering God's rest?

2. Are you born again?

3. How do you know if you are born again?

4. Are there any God-given promises you have a hard time holding on to?

DAY 28
DID YOU SAY OBEY

> *John 14:23*
>
> *"Jesus replied, "Anyone who loves me will obey my teaching. My Father will love them, and we will come to them and make our home with them."*

Today, we look at a word many people cringe when they hear. The word is obey. This word often carries a negative connotation, like obedience is a bad thing or something forced upon someone else. I have even had individuals ask me not to put the word obey in their marriage vows. This is problematic. The truth is, the more we view obedience negatively, the less we desire to obey God. Disobedience is the opposite of obedience; when we refuse to accept obedience in our relationship with the Lord, we are disobedient.

The passage today states, "Anyone who loves me will obey my teaching." We may need to reverse the statement to grasp the gravity of the Lord's words. If we were to say anyone who does not obey Jesus' teachings does not love Him, we might begin to grasp the importance of obeying the Lord. Very few people, if any, would dare say I don't love you, Jesus. The thought of those words coming from an individual's mouth is atrocious. Yet every day, when we live against the Lord's teachings, we are saying we don't love Him. By now, you should have begun to see there is no in-between place to be. We are either for Him or against Him, obedient or disobedient. We either love Him or we don't.

The passage continues with, "My Father will love them, and we will come to them, and make our home with them." This is a powerful statement. God Himself, in all His fullness, will come and make His home in you. This is something I have held on to in my life, and it is such an encouragement. All of us go through things. In fact, Scripture states we will have trouble in this life. That last statement probably comes as no surprise. A lot of the trouble we bring on ourselves is because of our disobedience, but even when we are obedient, we will still face adversity. The knowledge that God is living in and through me has given me the ability to know that no matter what, I will overcome. Nothing can stand against God or overcome him, and no sin can overtake Him. This means that in and through Him, I, too, will overcome.

The best part is, all it takes for victory is obedience. This may sound too elementary, but it is that simple. What I love about this truth is that we don't have to be super spiritual, knowledgeable, or even able to quote a bunch of Scripture to overcome. All we have to do is obey. We don't have to know how God will do it, why He will do it, or even the theology behind it. We only need to follow His marching orders, for the battle belongs to Him, not us.

The problem most people have is they've fooled themselves into believing they are obedient to God, love Jesus, and are right where they need to be. The problem with this is they are living for themselves, doing what they want, even though they know that it doesn't honor God or equate Holiness. They partake of the world and feed their flesh all along, living the lie of loving God. This cannot be. We know the Bible says, "No man can serve two masters: for either he will hate the one, and love the other; or else he will hold to the one, and despise the other. Ye cannot serve God and mammon." (KJV) Simply put, if you love Him, you will obey Him.

Changed

Day 28 Exercises

1. Does your life show that you love the Lord?

2. What teachings of Jesus do you find hard to follow?

3. What do you need to surrender to the Lord in order to be obedient?

4. With God making His home in you, list the things you can accomplish.

Week 5

> *"Admitting our problems, sins and shortcomings is the first step in overcoming them and finding victory."*

We have just spent the week looking at the things we've done, our thought processes, and our desires. We should have all realized by now we are not stuck doing the same old things over and over again. We don't have to make the same mistakes and go down the same paths. Change is not only possible; it is God's plan and desire to bring about the necessary changes. It has been said if we don't study history, it is bound to repeat itself. We must search deeply to prevent history from repeating itself and making the same old mistakes. Knowing where we've been and how we got there can teach us how not to go back. We must be honest with ourselves and others while searching our lives and taking this personal inventory. Part of finding victory is admitting our behaviors to our loved ones. For many of us, accepting responsibility is foreign, as we are used to blaming someone else for everything we do.

If we desire to be free, we must apply the Biblical principle of exposure to our lives. This principle is confessing our sins to God, self, and others, then repenting. Shame and guilt have caused us to avoid God, which has kept us bound to and entangled in our sins. Bombarding with shame and guilt is the same tactic the devil used in the Garden of Eden against Adam and Eve. He first deceived them and then tempted them to sin. After they sinned, he condemned them. He used shame and guilt to drive them from God. We may not have tried to hide from God by sewing fig leaves together, but we have followed in their footsteps. When we come face to face with our sins and behaviors, we not only hide from God but from others as well. We isolate, and in our isolation, the shame, guilt, and condemnation drive us to sin more, which drives us to dive deeper into the same behaviors. It is a vicious cycle that is impossible for us to break alone.

Adam and Eve did all they could to cover their sin and hide it from God, but their best efforts were futile and ineffective. This, too, describes us as most of us have done everything in our power to hide and disguise our sins and shortcomings, but this is the exact opposite of what we should do. Instead of running from God, we should run to Him. Instead of hiding our sins, we should expose them. As long as we hide them, they maintain control over us, but when we expose them, they lose their hold on us, and we can break free.

Changed

Ephesians 5:12-14 states: "It would be shameful even to mention here those pleasures of darkness that the ungodly do. But when you expose them, the light shines in upon their sin and shows it up, and when they see how wrong they are, some of them may even become children of light! That is why God says in the Scriptures, 'Awake, O sleeper, and rise up from the dead; and Christ shall give you light.'"(Living Bible) Those dark areas lose their hold on us when we expose them to the light of God. In the 12 steps, Step 5 is to admit to God, ourselves, and another human being the exact nature of our wrongs. Step 5 describes the act of confession, repentance, and accountability.

Coming face to face with who we are can be painful but necessary. Admitting to ourselves and taking responsibility is the act of confession. Admitting and rejecting our behaviors and sin to God is the repentance necessary for freedom. Finally, admitting the exact nature of our wrongs to another human being is to find the accountability we need to keep us from sliding back into a life of compromise. Enough compromise, and we will find ourselves right back where we started.

Don't sell yourself short by believing the lie that you can do this with no one's help. God did not design us to live alone. At creation, He made us as a pair. Then in the New Testament, when Jesus sent out His disciples, He sent them out two by two. We need accountability. We need fellowship. We need the entire body of Christ to be victorious in this life.

DAY 29
CONFESSION

> *Proverbs 28:13*
>
> *"Whoever conceals their sins does not prosper, but the one who confesses and renounces them finds mercy."*

No one likes to admit they are wrong, and as I have already stated, we are extremely good at blaming others for our problems. Even the thought of needing to approach someone to admit how you have wronged them and how our behavior has affected them makes most of us cringe in embarrassment and humiliation. Regardless of whether we admit it or not, we are prideful people who do not like to open up and lay ourselves bare.

Our passage today explains why most of us are in our current situation. It states, "Whoever conceals their sins does not prosper." Through the years, I have met many people who have asked me to pray for God to bless them and their current activities. Often, they ask me to request God's blessings over things God has clearly defined as disobedient behavior. One of the most frequent situations is for a couple who are unmarried and living together; they come to the altar and ask for prayer that God will bless their relationship. God can't bless what He has already condemned. While in this particular situation, they are not trying to conceal their behavior to hide what they are doing from the church. They are cloaking their sins with the blanket of acceptance by today's culture.

The principles of confessing and renouncing sin must be present in our lives to receive God's mercy. Even so, we must look beyond those secret sins we hide from everyone and search every area of our lives, looking for any area where our behavior, thoughts, or actions don't align with God's Word. All of these areas are what we must confess. This confession begins first to ourselves and then to God. We have to come to grips with the fact that what we are doing is wrong. Regardless of cultural norms, anything that is not within God's design for us is wrong and, therefore, is sin. Once we confess and renounce, we no longer need to conceal the matter no longer.

As previously discussed, when we admit to ourselves, God, and another human being, the things that once controlled us lose their grip, and we are set free. Once free, we can step out of a life that is going nowhere and, in turn, step into a life that is prosperous in the things which really matter. Those prosperous things are what God designed for us to walk in the moment He created us. Once we reject and renounce those things opposed to God, then God Himself fills us with His love, joy, peace, and patience.

With all the years we have been bound in guilt, crippled by condemnation, and unable to love ourselves, much less anyone else, I'm sure the idea of being free is unfathomable for some. Nonetheless, freedom is what we are promised, and freedom is what God will give. God's promises have no hidden strings attached to them. All of His promises become ours simply by being obedient to Him. This obedience can be summed up in four words: confess, repent, believe, and receive.

Changed

Day 29 Exercises

1. What behaviors and sins have you been concealing?

_____
_____
_____
_____
_____
_____
_____

2. Who do you need to reveal these things to and how has your secret sins affected you and others?

_____
_____
_____
_____
_____
_____
_____
_____

3. How do you feel about being set free from shame, guild and condemnation?

_____
_____
_____
_____
_____
_____
_____
_____

4. What does a prosperous life look like and how do you obtain it?

_____
_____
_____
_____
_____
_____
_____
_____

DAY 30
GUILTY

> *1 John 1:8*
>
> *"If we claim to be without sin, we deceive ourselves and the truth is not in us."*

Today's passage seems to be stating what is straightforward and obvious. The majority of us already know we are sinners and wouldn't think about trying to deny it. After all, we know Scripture states that "we all have sinned and fallen short of the Glory of God." Even though this passage seems straightforward, and none of us may actively deny that we are sinners, this verse still applies to each of us. We must look at a few things to fully understand how to apply today's passage to our lives.

First, God's ways are not our ways. Second, God is the same yesterday, today, and forever. Third, only God defines Holiness and Righteousness. Society may define what is currently acceptable in cultural practices, but society doesn't define what is unacceptable to God. Too many of our everyday activities dishonor Him. To correctly apply today's passage, we will address those areas society calls acceptable and Scripture is clearly against. If we are ever going to become the person God created us to be, we must be honest with ourselves and God. While most of us may not claim to be "without sin," many of us feel what we do is okay. Even if we readily admit many of our behaviors don't honor God, we, on some level, feel they don't dishonor Him either. We tend to treat our lives like a smorgasbord, picking and choosing certain areas of our lives to conform to His Word while ignoring others. The more areas we surrender to Him the better we feel about ourselves and our relationship with God, and the closer we feel we are to being who He created us to be.

Unfortunately, we deceive ourselves because if we don't surrender every area to the Lord, we are still far from reaching His plan for our lives. The truth is, most "Christians" have no interest in fully surrendering and living a Holy life. We have entertained the world's fleshly desires for so long and have compromised His standard for what the world tells us is acceptable and right. In reality, these two don't mix. When we try to live in both worlds, we lie, and the truth is not in us. A life that seems to honor God yet still finds the fleshly desires of this world acceptable is not a God-honoring life. We are called to live a life worthy of our calling and to be Holy because He is Holy.

This means no one can be right with God and accept the ways of the world. As today's passage states, we lie. We lie to ourselves when we decide what is right and wrong. When we decide, the truth is not in us. Regardless of what we do right, if we knowingly participate in what the Bible defines as sin, we are guilty of breaking the law. The Scriptures state in James 2:10, "For whoever keeps the whole law and yet stumbles at just one point is guilty of breaking all of it." This is why it is so essential for each of us to examine our lives deeply and thoroughly. We must ensure we don't stop short and end up a lukewarm individual that God will reject. The only way to hear "well done, my good and faithful servant" is to do well and to be good and faithful. There is no in-between. We will either hear "Well done" or "Depart from me" (Matthew 25). First John 2:15 states, "Do not love the world or anything in the world. If anyone loves the world, love for the Father is not in them." Accepting or loving the world's things and claiming we are right with God is only to deceive ourselves.

Changed

Day 30 Exercises

1. List areas that are acceptable socially but unacceptable to God?

___

2. What areas are you guilty of lying about?

___

3. What must you reject to be right with God?

___

4. Explain in detail what your life would look like free from the areas we have been discussing today?

___

DAY 31
I'M SORRY

> *2 Corinthians 7:10*
>
> *"Godly sorrow brings repentance that leads to salvation and leaves no regret, but worldly sorrow brings death."*

Expressing sorrow, being sorry, overcoming regret, apologizing, and giving forgiveness are all things much easier to say than to do. Today, our text defines two types of sorrow: Godly sorrow and worldly sorrow. It tells us that Godly sorrow will lead to salvation and worldly sorrow to death. One is good for us, and the other isn't. Godly sorrow is deep conviction and sadness for violating God's will. It goes beyond being sad for moral failure, illegal activity, or even violation of Biblical standards. Godly sorrow may include all of these, but it will also include any offense, straying, or seeking one's own will above God's.

Sorrow is beyond sadness and even regret. The difference between sadness and sorrow is like the difference between sympathy and empathy. Sympathy is to be compassionate and understanding of what someone is going through. To have empathy, we are not only compassionate and understanding of one's experiences, but we also connect to their experience and feel what they are feeling. No one can empathize with someone without having sympathy, but you can express sympathy without actually having empathy. The same is true for sorrow. In order to be sorrowful, we must first be sorry, but just because we are sorry does not mean we have become sorrowful. Godly sorrow is to move beyond sadness and regret for our actions and reach a place where we can understand how our offense has broken God's heart. When we finally recognize and accept how much pain and sadness our behavior has inflicted on ourselves, others, and God, sorrow will follow. When we reach Godly sorrow, by understanding the impact of our sin, it becomes virtually impossible for us to "backslide," "slip up," or "accidentally" go back to the same old behaviors. Godly sorrow is a must for real change to take place. Godly sorrow must be reached for us to repent, transform, and find salvation.

I often think of Paul when he was on the road to Damascus. He wasn't a bad guy. Unlike many of us, he was determined to keep the law fully, willing to do anything necessary to be in right standing with God. Even so, with his best intentions, he was still acting in opposition to God's will. This made him a sinner, a lawbreaker who was out of God's will. Most of us can fully relate to being a sinner and living outside of God's will for our lives. Unlike Paul, in most cases, our ability to relate wasn't for trying to seek righteousness but pleasure. It is important to note that seeking to be righteous with our own strength, ability, and understanding will always fail. In and of ourselves, it is impossible to meet God's standard. The more we try, the further we end up from where we need to be. This was Paul. With everything he was, he gave it his all to be set apart, holy, and right with God. In his zeal, he actually was fighting against God and His plan. God met him while on his way to hunt down more of Jesus' followers and bring them to justice. Once he met God personally and realized how wrong he had been, he experienced and expressed Godly sorrow. This sorrow caused him to repent and turn from his current lifestyle. He gave up his ideas of righteousness, his personal agenda, and even his desires to be used by God. He found eternal life and eternal purpose. When we stop being sorry for what we have been doing, just because we don't like the consequences, and truly repent because of how much our actions have hurt God, we will find the life God designed for us.

Changed

Day 31 Exercises

1. Explain the difference between worldly sorrow and Godly sorrow.

2. How have your sinful choices impacted those close to you?

3. In what ways have you broken God's heart?

4. Write a prayer to God expressing your feelings about the life you have been living.

DAY 32
POWER IN PRAYER

> *James 5:16*
>
> *"Therefore confess your sins to each other and pray for each other so that you may be healed. The prayer of a righteous person is powerful and effective."*

There is an expression that states: "Confession is good for the soul." Many people have quoted this statement without realizing it is based on the Biblical passage above. Today's text states: "The prayer of a righteous person is powerful and effective." As we studied yesterday, righteousness can't be found in our own strength. It must come from God living in and through us. Understanding this puts it all into perspective. Often, we feel our prayers are going nowhere; like God just isn't listening and it is useless even to make the request. This is because we are missing the most crucial part of our prayer life—the Lord Himself. Without God, our prayers are just words, sometimes eloquent but nonetheless just ineffective words.

We don't need more words, fancier speech, or a specific position for God to hear and move on behalf of our prayers. What we need is His Spirit within us. His Spirit residing in us is righteousness. His Spirit will lead us in what and how to pray, and when we pray according to His will, we can know those prayers are effective and powerful. The effectiveness is on God, not on us. We are unable and inadequate. In fact, we are all sinners and fall short of God's Glory. Only by applying the first part of our text today, confessing, can we reach powerful and effective prayers. We are told to confess our sins to one another and to pray for each other. Confession is not entering a private room and talking to a specific person about sins we are guilty of committing. Confession first starts with the Godly sorrow we studied yesterday. That sorrow leads to repentance. Repentance and confession must go together. Confession is recognizing, admitting, and sharing the wrongs we are guilty of. In order for repentance to happen, confession must take place. We must first admit to God we are wrong, we are sinners, and then repent.

In repentance, we must turn away from our sinful behaviors and live completely opposite lifestyles to that which we have repented of. When our lives take on this new direction, we are changed. This change in and of itself is a form of confession. Our changed life's actions, behaviors, and desires are confessing that our previous actions were wrong. Becoming His and being transformed is the most important part of confession and repentance, but today's passage even takes it further. Today we read that we are to confess to one another and pray for each other. Many people try to adopt an attitude that portrays their relationship with God as an individual thing. They believe their relationship with God is nobody else's business and feel no one should have to answer to anybody but God. This simply is not true. Over and over again throughout the Bible, we see God did not design for us to handle life on our own terms. Adam was not left alone in this world, and even when Jesus sent out His disciples, He did so two by two. We are commanded not to forsake the gathering together for fellowship, and we are instructed that it takes each part of the body of Christ to work together the way He designed.

This is why we are reminded here to confess to one another. We find accountability and strength when we share our struggles and confess to other believers. When we open up to others, they know how to pray for us and encourage us, and we know how to do the same for them. This confessing to others and repenting is vital to our walk with God and vital to the righteous life we desire. There is strength in numbers, and regardless of how close we may be with Christ at this moment in our lives, there will come a time when we need the body of Christ, fellow believers, to help strengthen our walk.

Day 32 Exercises

1. Have you been guilty of half-hearted repentance? If so, why? Explain what has been holding you back.

2. Do your desires line up with God's Word?

3. How do you fall short when comparing yourself to Jesus?

4. What are you proud about in your life?

DAY 33
DISCLOSED

> *Luke 8:17*
>
> *"For there is nothing hidden that will not be disclosed, and nothing concealed that will not be known or brought out into the open."*

Many of us have experienced today's verse in some way or another. "There is nothing hidden that will not be disclosed and nothing concealed that will not be known or brought out into the open." Every one of us are sinners. None of us are without fault. We have spent a lifetime doing what we want, pleasing ourselves, and satisfying our fleshly desires. This self-seeking living is often morally wrong, illegal, and hurtful to others.

When these desires conflict with what is expected of us, we hide our sins and live a facade instead of making the necessary changes. The worst part of this double lifestyle is the only person we are effectively fooling is ourselves. More often than not, our family and friends already know what we are doing.

I know this has been true in my own life. No matter how careful I thought I was or how good I thought I was at hiding my bad choices, those closest to me most often already knew. Even if I was successful for a while at hiding my behaviors, eventually, they would surface and usually in such a way that was embarrassing and with devastating effects. The truth is, if I had been successful in pretending to be someone I'm not, I would have accomplished nothing. My life was still in a mess; my soul was in turmoil, and God knew everything I had done.

Knowing and accepting that what we do in secret will be revealed should be a huge motivating factor to not participate in shameful behaviors. Unfortunately, our flesh nature always makes us believe it won't happen to us. This is a lie from the enemy. We must understand God cannot lie. His Words are true, and what He has declared will come to pass. This means every deceitful, shameful, unethical, immoral, and sinful decision will be made known.

The Good News is that God desires to set us free regardless of what we have done. It doesn't matter how bad, hurtful or even how long we have been involved with our sins, God still desires to free us. He longs for us to repent, to turn away from those shameful things, and turn to Him. Imagine the freedom of living a life that requires no deceit, secrets, or pretending; a life where you can be real to yourself, others, and God.

When we finally make the decision to come to God and give our lives to Christ, we will find a life that no longer requires us to look over our shoulders and wonder if anyone knows what we are doing. When we surrender to Him, we will find the life we have always longed for, a life full of peace and purpose. We will live free of guilt and shame. We can be confident because a life lived in Christ will no longer need to hide behaviors, live secretly, or pretend.

Changed

Day 33 Exercises

1. Describe the difficulty in hiding your secret sins(s)? What lengths have you employed to keep your sinful lifestyle hidden?

_____
_____
_____
_____
_____
_____
_____
_____

2. What sinful lifestyles have you overcome?

_____
_____
_____
_____
_____
_____
_____
_____

3. Why is it impossible to be right with God while actively participating in unrighteousness?

_____
_____
_____
_____
_____
_____
_____
_____

4. If you surrender the areas you are struggling with to the Lord, what will happen?

_____
_____
_____
_____
_____
_____
_____
_____

DAY 34
TRUTH

> *John 8:32*
>
> *"Then you will know the truth, and the truth will set you free."*

Truth. What is truth? Today's culture would have us believe truth is relative. You may have even heard statements like "that is your truth" or "that is your reality." The problem with this thought process is there are not multiple truths or realities. There is the truth, and everything else is a lie. From a young age, we are taught to think for ourselves, act on our emotions, and figure things out on our own. This independent lifestyle is not what God designed. In fact, it is the exact opposite. We were designed to be dependent on God. We must realize our heart is deceitful, our emotions fluctuate, and our understanding is limited. We simply don't see the whole picture. We don't know the future or even the results of our actions. God, on the other hand, sees and knows all. He knows the truth.

If we are seeking truth, we must realize it can't be found in anything other than God Himself. Our passage today states, "Then you will know the truth, and the truth shall set you free." The question is, what is the "then" in this verse? What must take place for us to know the truth and then be set free by it? In John 8, Jesus states in verses 31 and 32: "'If you hold to my teaching, you are really my disciples. Then you will know the truth, and the truth will set you free.'" The only way to know God and know the truth is to hold to His teachings. John 14:15 explains that if we love Him, we will obey Him. This lifestyle of obedience will cause us to hold to His teaching, and we will know the truth because we know Him.

The end result of a lifestyle of obedience and love toward Jesus is a free life; a life free from the bondage of sin, free from addiction, and free from a life of immorality. It may be hard to imagine a life that is free from guilt and condemnation, but in Christ, this is exactly what we receive. The truth is God loves us so much He paid the penalty for our sins through Christ's sacrifice on the cross. We do not receive forgiveness in Christ because we are innocent or even because we are good people. We receive forgiveness by God's grace because of His great love for us.

Every sin we have ever committed must be atoned. This means to make good on it, to pay the debt owed for each of those sins. The Bible tells us what we deserve and earn for our sins is death. This simply means the price for each and every one of our sins will be paid. They will be paid for by either us or Christ. Unfortunately, as imperfect humans full of sin and controlled by the flesh's nature, we can't satisfy the requirements. This, in turn, puts us in a perpetual state of eternal death, attempting to pay the penalty of our sins for eternity. Only the sacrifice of the perfect, sinless Son of God can fulfill the debt and make it paid in full.

Changed

Day 34 Exercises

1. What does being free mean to you?

_____
_____
_____
_____
_____
_____
_____
_____

2. What has your sin cost you?

_____
_____
_____
_____
_____
_____
_____
_____
_____

3. Are there any areas of you life that are not exemplifying the teachings of Jesus?

_____
_____
_____
_____
_____
_____
_____
_____
_____

4. What will your life look like completely surrendered to the Lord?

_____
_____
_____
_____
_____
_____
_____
_____
_____

DAY 35
PURIFIED

> *1 John 1:9*
>
> *"If we confess our sins, he is faithful and just and will forgive us our sins and purify us from all unrighteousness."*

Knowing we have a debt to God we cannot pay and understanding we must be born again brings us to our verse today. In review, we have come to understand that our way doesn't work. We now know that only God can change us. He is the only One who can fix what is broken and transform us from being driven by our sinful flesh nature to being led by His Spirit. We should have taken a long, hard look at all the areas we have fallen short of God's design for us, and prayerfully, we each have experienced life-changing salvation.

Today, we will discuss a new component of God's transforming power. God clearly is the One who has done all the work for our freedom. He is the One who designed and created us. He is the One who paved the way for our forgiveness, and He is the One who provided the means for our salvation. It is God who has done it all. Today's passage defines our part in all of this. We know it takes at least two individuals for a covenant or contract to be established, and each party has particular responsibilities within a contract. The best part of our covenant with God is that He has provided us with all the necessary means to fulfill our responsibilities. Nothing He requires of us is unobtainable. In fact, believe it or not, our side of this covenant is easily executed if we will but just obey.

We can simplify our part by recognizing it starts with confessing. Just as 1 John 1:9 states: "If we confess our sins, He is faithful and just and will forgive us our sins and purify us from all unrighteousness." Again, it is God who has provided and fulfilled all the necessary requirements. The only thing we must do is confess. Now, this is where so many get it wrong. The confession described here is not just an admittance of wrongdoing. Most of us have no problem realizing we have been wrong, done wrong, and even lived wrong. The issue comes in what confession means.

To confess is to come in agreement with God and His Word that His righteous requirements are right. We must first recognize that our way has been wrong. Then, when we confess, we must move beyond just agreeing in word. For instance, if I confess smoking is wrong, that it does not glorify God, and that it does not honor His temple, admitting this, knowing it, and yet continuing to smoke all the while is not real confessing. True confession also includes repentance.

Repentance is to do a complete 180. It means we stop what we have admitted and do the opposite. Returning to our current illustration, if I admit smoking is a sin and I confess that to the Lord, for confession to have taken place, I must repent of my actions, turn from them, and seek God's help and guidance not to fall back to that sinful behavior. When confession takes place, "He is faithful and just and will forgive us our sins and purify us from all unrighteousness."

Changed

Day 35 Exercises

1. What sins in your life do you need to confess?

_____
_____
_____
_____
_____
_____
_____
_____

2. Why would or wouldn't it be hard to turn from these sins?

_____
_____
_____
_____
_____
_____
_____
_____

3. What does God want you to do with these behaviors?

_____
_____
_____
_____
_____
_____
_____
_____

4. Is there any reason why God wouldn't cleanse you from all your unrighteousness?

_____
_____
_____
_____
_____
_____
_____
_____

Week 6

> *"The Creator defines the creation, creation does not define the Creator."*

Who are you? When asked this question, most people will answer by telling you what they do. They will begin to list their careers as if that is what defines who they are. You may hear people say they are a carpenter, an electrician, a dancer, a photographer, and so forth. They may work in carpentry or any other careers listed above, yet, if they stopped working in that field, they would still be the same person. If you retire or can't continue to function in a particular career, your real identity doesn't change. You are still the same person. What you do does not make you who you are.

Usually, the following thought process is for an individual to try and answer the question, who are you, with their cultural or religious views. For instance, some will list their denomination, religious beliefs, or heritage, such as Baptist, Methodist, Buddhist, Jewish, atheist, and more. Again, if you change churches or join a non-denominational church after belonging to a Baptist church, does that action change who you are? The answer is, of course, no. So, who are we? What makes us who we are, and how can we fully know who we are? When we can answer this question wholeheartedly, we will find that who we are defines what we do. It is not what we do that defines who we are. I firmly believe "when you know who you are, you know what to do."

Understanding who we are becomes a top priority when looking to make necessary changes in our lives. Since we are not what we do, our careers, hobbies, or even our style of worship, how do we know who we are? The answer to this is found where it all started, in the very beginning, in the creation account. As with anything, the one who designs it knows what it is, what it was designed to do, and why it was designed. This is true for us, too. We have a Designer, God, who created us for a purpose, and only the Designer can define us.

In Genesis 1:26, God states: "Let us make mankind in our image, in our likeness." In this passage, God the Father is speaking to Jesus and the Holy Spirit. Paying attention to what is said gives us our first glimpse of who we are. Then, in the same verse, God declares why He created us. It states: "so that they may rule over the fish in the sea and the birds in the sky, over the livestock and all the wild animals, and over all the creatures that move along the ground." God created us to rule the Earth for Him. He created us to have dominion over fish, birds, livestock, wild animals, and all other creatures that move along the ground."

Changed

We were created in God's image and in His likeness for His purpose. If you read the account of the rest of creation, you will see that God spoke to the waters, and upon His word, the waters teamed with life of all varying kinds. God spoke to the land, and it produced vegetation of all kinds. Again God spoke to the land, and it brought forth creatures of varying kinds, and so forth.

Pay attention now, to the sea creatures being brought forth from the sea. When they die, they return to that from which they came, the sea. When the creatures of the Earth die, they return to that from which they were made, the Earth. Since mankind is made from the dust of the earth in God's image and in His likeness, when we die we too return to that from which we were created. Just as God is a triune existence in the Father, Son, and Holy Spirit, with the Three being One, we, being made in His image, also have a triune existence. We are made in flesh, soul, and Spirit. In our original design, the flesh will return to the dust from which it was created, and our soul and Spirit will return to that from which it was made, God Himself.

Knowing that we are made in God's image, given His Spirit, and that He designed our soul to be eternally with Him makes us wonder how we could ever struggle and need change. The answer to that question is also found in Genesis. We need change because sin entered the world. Until that moment, mankind ruled the Earth and worked the garden for the Lord. We had an eternal existence and were connected directly to God by His Spirit. Once sin entered the world, that sin broke the fellowship we had with God, and mankind became spiritually dead.

This missing part is why almost everyone has felt that empty spot within. We try to fill that void with all kinds of things except the one "thing" that can actually fill it. Instead of being complete, we are simply flesh and soul. This is why the flesh nature drives all of us and why we fall so far from what God had designed for us. When we believe and receive Jesus as our Savior, we are born again.

Being born again transforms us and literally gives us back the missing piece we desperately need. Upon accepting Christ, we are filled with His Spirit and brought back to our original design of flesh, soul, and Spirit. Having been reconciled to God, renewed by His Spirit, and empowered by His presence, we can step into that which God has designed for us. We can live a life of victory, ability, and dominion. This means with His Spirit, we can exercise complete rule over everything in this life. Without the transformation of being born again, we cannot exercise the dominion and rule God designed for us to walk in. In fact, in our spiritually dead state, instead of ruling, we are ruled, controlled, and led by our flesh nature, and this is why we need God to change our lives.

DAY 36
IN HIS IMAGE

> *Genesis 1:26*
>
> *"Then God said, "Let us make mankind in our image, in our likeness, so that they may rule over the fish in the sea and the birds in the sky, over the livestock and all the wild animals, and over all the creatures that move along the ground."*

You are not an accident. Whether your parents planned you or you were a surprise to them, you are not an accident. None of us chose to be born, asked to exist, or even planned our arrival. The time in which we came to be was not our choosing nor our parents. Even if your parents carefully planned all the timing for you to be here, it still was not up to them. Unexpected or expected, neither one matters because none of us can be born except by the will of God. Life, creation, and purpose belong to Him and Him alone.

No matter what you have been told your whole life, God desired for you to be born, or you would not have been. The enemy would like us all to believe we exist by happenstance or by our parents' will, but that simply isn't true. We exist because God planned us. To carry this truth a bit further, neither ourselves, our parents, nor our family members designed us. They did not choose what we would excel in or what we may be deficient in. Our parents did not decide anything about who we are. Our family is only responsible for how their sins and decisions have affected our development. They did not create us.

It is important to grasp that God is the only One who can create. The enemy cannot create, nor can anyone or anything else. The only thing the enemy can do is pervert what God has created. For example, God created sex. It is the enemy that perverted it. The same is true with us. God created us, He designed us, and He knows the purpose for which He planned for us. We are not broken. We have every ability God designed us to have. If there is anything that seems amiss, it is because we have allowed the enemy to pervert what God brought forth.

Many who read this devotion may have some type of life-controlling issues. You may have an addiction that has controlled your life for many years, one that you have tried desperately to overcome time and time again, only to return to the same old things. The enemy would have you believe that your situation is unchangeable and that you will forever be stuck in these behaviors and sins. The enemy's desire is for you to think something is wrong with you and that you need to get rid of the addictive personality you have. I don't believe this to be the case. In fact, I believe it is God that gave us this personality trait. Those with addictive personalities will leave their houses, jobs, families, and everything for what they love.

I believe God created those with addictive personalities to be sold out for Him. Only those with this type of personality will leave everything for Him. Those with this character trait become missionaries, teachers, pastors, and evangelists. God created us this way, but by our own free will and generational influences, the enemy perverted it. Instead of being sold out for our Savior, we sold out for substances, for something less than He designed. We don't need to get rid of this trait but allow God to bring it back to His original purpose.

Changed

Day 36 Exercises

1. What traits do you think may have been perverted by the enemy in your life?

2. What do you believe God desires to do in and through you?

3. What does it mean to be created by God in His image?

4. Since God has a purpose for all of His creations, what is your purpose?

DAY 37
ON MY SIDE

> *Romans 8:31*
>
> *"What, then, shall we say in response to these things? If God is for us, who can be against us?"*

Each of us has been designed and created by God with His purposes in mind. We are His, and when we surrender to Him and get right with Him, He is on our side. I don't think most of us grasp what it means to have God on our side. He is not only our Creator; He is the Creator of the entire universe. He is the One who spoke, "Let there be light," and there was light. He took that which did not exist, and by His spoken Word, everything came to be. He is the same God that kept Shadrach, Meshach, and Abednego from getting even a hair singed in that raging furnace. He is the same God that shut the mouths of the lions when Daniel was thrown into the lion's den, and He is the same God that enabled and instructed Noah to build the Ark that saved creation and Noah's family.

Understanding the power and ability that rest within our God is essential in facing everything we will go through here on Earth. Today's passage sums up the reality that if God is on our side, there is nothing and no one who can be against us. There really is nothing we cannot accomplish, nothing we cannot overcome, and nothing that can defeat us. We have every tool and resource we need to overcome whatever we may face. We will prevail, we will succeed, and we will get through whatever comes our way. None of it will be by our might, our ability, or even by our own strength, but in Christ, with Him on our side, we will succeed.

The enemy would have us believe we are stuck the way we are, and there is no hope for change. He will use past failed attempts and anything else to make us believe we are bound to fail. We must remember that the enemy is a liar. Everything he says is a lie, and he can't be believed. Every lie must have an element of truth to it for it to be believable. It may be true that in the past, we have tried to overcome or make changes and have failed, but it is a complete lie to believe we are stuck that way and cannot overcome. While it may be true that in our own power, we are incapable, we can overcome anything and everything with God on our side. Smoking was one of the things I was finally able to overcome, even though I failed many times before. I jokingly say quitting smoking is easy, and I would know, I did it eight times. Of course, that means I failed seven times. The difference in my last attempt to quit that finally brought success was not quitting in my own strength but God's. My reason for quitting also changed the last and final time. I quit simply so my life could bring honor to my Lord and Savior.

With this as my motive and with my whole heart seeking to glorify God, I was finally able to be a non-smoker. Now let me say this: it wasn't that it was any easier to quit. I didn't supernaturally no longer desire to smoke, nor did I stop craving nicotine. What was different was with God's help: whenever I was tempted, or the enemy tried to make me think I couldn't do it, I stayed focused on God's ability to see me through it. Just as I was able to focus on His ability to see me through each and every day, so can you. What He has been able to do in me, He can do in you. He is on your side, and you can do what He desires you to do.

Changed

Day 37 Exercises

1. What have you tried to change in your life but have failed?

___

2. Explain why God may be limited to help you change?

___

3. Describe what your life would look like with God helping you.

___

4. What will be different for you this time?

___

DAY 38
ALL THINGS

> *Romans 8:28*
>
> *"And we know that in all things God works for the good of those who love him, who have been called according to his purpose."*

Today's passage boldly states, "All things work for the good." If we are honest, the idea that all things work for good is far more than just unbelievable. The truth is when we take today's verse at face value, it can even be considered offensive. So many individuals question how the tragic things they have been through are good. The problem is the misinterpretation of the verse. They change it to say all things are good. This verse does not say all things are good. What it says is that God works all things together for the good. After declaring God's ability to work everything together for good, today's verse gives pre-qualifiers that must be met for God to accomplish this. Those pre-qualifications are loving Him and being called according to His purpose.

The first pre-qualifier is to love Him. To love God, we must first know Him. So many people fall in love with the idea of love or even the idea of an individual they deem lovable. We tend to fall in love with what we want someone to be, not who they actually are. Building relationships on the "idea" of someone and not the reality of who they are, will always disappoint. The attraction to that individual will be built on false pretense, and it will crumble. This happens Spiritually, too. Many people claim to love God and to be committed to Him. Yet, when God responds or leads in a manner that doesn't meet their expectations, their relationship with God crumbles. In order to love anyone, really love them, we must know them. The same is true for God; in order to really love Him, we must know Him, spend time with Him, and read His Word. This will build a relationship that won't crumble under the pressures of life but will rest in the assurance that He is working all things together for good.

You see, when we love God, we will put Him first. This is actually the number one commandment, to love God "with all your heart and with all your soul and with all your mind and with all your strength" (Mark 12:30). When we love God, we will desire Him, we will long for righteousness and His Holiness. Love honors, Love respects, Love gives, and the Word of God says that if we love Him, we will obey Him (John 14:15). The second qualifier is to be called according to His purpose. This is the easiest part because we have nothing to do with it. This calling is all God's work. Yes, we love Him because He first loved us, but as we have seen already, to love Him requires active obedience on our part. Being called requires no active work on our part. God is the One who calls, and God is the One who establishes the purpose of that call. The call here is an official call that demands action, much like a subpoena. We must answer this call or suffer the consequences of rejecting it. As to the purpose, we can rest assured that regardless of the current circumstances, God's ultimate purpose is to "prosper us and not to harm us, to give us a hope and a future" (Jer. 29:11).

I know I have been called, and I know God has a purpose for me. I have committed my life to loving Him, so I have found assurance and peace knowing that this verse is true. I have often reminded myself that His Word is true and claim this passage of Scripture in my life. When going through all the hard things that life puts us through, when the unexplainable happens and we are shaken to the core, we can know that God is still in control and will work it all out in the end. I thank God that He has revealed the why behind many of the things I have been through. For those things I am still going through, I can rest in the assurance that God will see me through it, and if need be, he will reveal the purpose of those things.

Changed

Day 38 Exercises

1. Share two experiences you initially thought were bad but now see how God has worked for good

2. How does today's passage affect how you feel about your life right now?

3. List the areas you are dependent on God to work out for the good.

4. Write a prayer asking God to increase your faith to walk through life in the confidence that He is in control and that He has your best interest at heart.

DAY 39
MY CHOICE

> *Romans 8:29*
>
> *"For those God foreknew he also predestined to be conformed to the image of his Son, that he might be the firstborn among many brothers and sisters."*

Some define predestination as the idea that things are set, they are unchangeable, and that it doesn't matter what you do in life because your end is set in stone. I even once read of an individual who was walking out of church one Sunday after the service. As they were exiting the building, they tripped and fell. After suffering a sprung ankle and a skinned knee, the individual slowly rose from the ground with some assistance. After standing upright, he turned to the pastor and stated: "I'm glad that is finally over. I've been waiting my whole life for that to happen."

The above understanding of predestination is certainly one way to perceive it, but fortunately, this is not what God is saying here. Remember, God has given each of us free will choice. He has not made us robots. God could have made us all without a will, desires, and the ability to choose, but He didn't. His desire is for us to love Him because we choose to do so. It can only be sincere love and respect when we choose to do so on our own. There is no honor in us loving God if we have no choice.

A better understanding of this passage is to see how it goes hand in hand with John 6:37: "All those the Father gives me will come to me, and whoever comes to me I will never drive away." The predestination spoken of here is not a "predefined" everything is set and cannot be changed situation. The predestination spoken of here is the predetermined design by God for those who come to Jesus to be like Him. God designed us to be a part of His family, to be like His Son. God desires to be our Father and for us to be His children. He predestined us to be in a relationship with Him. He does not desire for us just to be an acquaintance. He longs for us to have a close, intimate, and personal relationship with Him, a relationship where we confidently know we are truly loved and a desired member of the family.

The Scripture today also states: "for those God foreknew." This foreknowledge, again, is not a predetermined state of election that chooses some and rejects others. The foreknowledge spoken of corresponds to God's all-knowing ability, His Omniscience. God already has the knowledge of who will and will not accept the call of the Holy Spirit to be born again. Those whom He knows will make the choice to accept Christ as their Savior are those whom He foreknows. Only those whom He knows will use their free will choice to choose Jesus. Those who choose Jesus are those who are "predestined to be conformed to the image of His Son."

One of the enemy's biggest tricks to defeat us is to make us believe that we are too far gone, that God has given up on us and that we are not His chosen. The enemy knows if we believe we won't be accepted, we will continue to live the life we have always lived, and we will never choose Jesus. Let me encourage you: if you are reading this now, it isn't too late. God wouldn't waste His time drawing you, calling you, and encouraging you to choose Him if you were already destined to be rejected. Second Peter 3:9 tells us that God wishes none to perish but for all to come to repentance. This means you, too. It is your free will choice.

Changed

Day 39 Exercises

1. Why have I been choosing to live by my own understanding?

2. What would my life look like if I were to be like Jesus?

3. What has God predetermined for me?

4. How will I show God that I love Him and that I am part of His family?

DAY 40
PRESSING ON

> *Philippians 3:12*
>
> *"Not that I have already obtained all this, or have already arrived at my goal, but I press on to take hold of that for which Christ Jesus took hold of me."*

Life is a constant journey. No matter what area in life we are talking about: spiritually, financially, or even physically, no one ever reaches a point where they have arrived. Sure, we may meet some goals, but as we all know, once we have accomplished our original goals, we tend to set additional goals. We are constantly evolving, growing and changing. At times, these adjustments are for the better, and sometimes they aren't. Understanding that we are not supposed to reach a point of arrival is extremely important, especially Spiritually speaking. You see, if we mistakingly believe we are to reach a point of completion when we fall short, we may feel that we have failed. The feelings of failure turn to despair, and that, in turn, causes us to give up and stop trying. All of this is a trick of the enemy to render us Spiritually crippled and distant from God.

In contrast, today's passage specifies that we are called to press on. This means we are on a continued path of growth and not trying to reach a point of Spiritual maturity and completion. Instead of trying to finish a task, we should take each day as an opportunity to grow and "take hold of" all that Christ came to give us. The great part of "pressing on" is the freedom we are afforded to correct our missteps. Each day serves as a new opportunity to do better and / or more. Falling short today is not the final state of our being.

The other truth within this verse that we must address is that we are not pressing on to something that is out of reach or unobtainable. We understand that as believers, we are called to be Holy, live a Righteous life, and conform to Christ's image. The problem is, the life we have lived within the flesh nature has been everything but Holy and Righteous. Habits, fleshly desires, and memories constantly pull at us and remind us of just how far from Christ we have been. If that were not bad enough, the enemy throws those experiences and memories at us all along, telling us we will never be able to become what God desires of us.

While I will readily admit, in and of ourselves, there is no way we can reach the Holy, Righteous, and Christ-like life, today's verse tells us plainly that we aren't called to do it ourselves. In fact, it states that Christ already took hold of it for us. You see, he has already claimed it. The life He designed for us has already been obtained. Jesus paid the price for it with His sacrifice on the cross. Not only is this God-designed life obtainable, it is expected. We simply must "press on." Every day, we simply have to strive toward the life that Christ paid the price for.

The mark of success again isn't to have arrived but to be pressing on, moving forward each and every day, drawing closer and closer. Small and minute changes within each of us and large and significant transformations are all a measure of victory. So today and each day forward, we must simply "press on," seeking and allowing Christ to transform us with what He already has waiting for us.

Changed

Day 40 Exercises

1. How do you feel about the idea that we are not seeking to arrive but to press on?

2. What are you pressing on towards?

3. What specifically do you need to surrender to press on?

4. What does it mean to you that Christ has already paid for your Righteousness and Holiness?

DAY 41
UNDIVIDED

> *Ezekiel 11:19*
>
> *"I will give them an undivided heart and put a new spirit in them; I will remove from them their heart of stone and give them a heart of flesh."*

God is promising to give us a changed heart in today's passage. With all that God has done for us why have we been so resistant to Him? His plans are better than ours and His love for us is greater than the love we have for ourselves. Our constant struggle and resistance to God's will is because our hearts are divided. We are torn between our flesh nature with all its generational influences and the deep longing our souls have to fill the void in our hearts. That God-sized hole longs to be made right with Him, to be victorious over sin, and to live a Holy life. Having a divided heart is not abnormal. It is how each and every one of us begins this journey of life. Every single one of us has battled with that Biblical conundrum; The Spirit indeed is willing, but the flesh is weak (Matthew 26:41). This battle is so prevalent that Paul deeply discusses this in Romans chapter 7. Here, Paul describes doing what he hates to do and not doing what he really wants. He summarizes his personal feelings in verse 24: "What a wretched man I am! Who will rescue me from this body of death?" We see from Paul's words that even those most dedicated and consistent in their service to the Lord have struggled with a divided heart. The Good News is that Paul's divided heart was changed. He did overcome, but it wasn't by his own power. He was an overcomer through Jesus Christ.

The promise is that God Himself will give us an undivided heart. Our verse today declares how God is able to change our hearts. It states, "I will put a new Spirit in them." Receiving this new Spirit is what happens the moment we surrender to God and accept Christ as our Savior. Paul goes on to explain the transition from a divided heart to an undivided heart in Romans chapter eight, starting in verse three and continuing to the end of the chapter. In short, it explains that God sent Jesus as a sacrifice for our sins so the penalty of the law would be fulfilled. Paul then shares how we are no longer bound to the flesh realm when the Spirit of God lives in us. All of this is done by the hand of God. We don't have to muster it up, figure it out, or even understand it. It is God that will put a new Spirit in us, it is God that will give us an undivided heart, and it is God that will change our hard and bitter heart to one that is full of compassion and love. Our only responsibility in any of this is to simply believe. We only need to live by faith that what God has promised, He will do. The more we spend time with God, reading our Bibles, praying, and resting in His presence, the more we will recognize the Spirit's work in our lives and the less we will resist Him.

I can testify this is exactly what God did in my life. I remember a time in my life when I didn't care much about anyone other than myself. I wasn't a bad guy, but I didn't care anything about you if I didn't know you. I certainly wasn't concerned about any stranger's eternity or where they would spend it. My heart was hard; I was selfish, and even though I didn't know it then, my heart was divided. I wanted to go to Heaven, I wanted to be right with God, but I didn't want to surrender my will to Him. After being broken, recognizing my wrongs, and getting right with God, my life is now devoted to helping strangers find salvation and freedom through a right relationship with Jesus. God changed me. He did it, not me, and if you will simply believe, He will do the same for you. God Himself will put His Spirit within you, and His Spirit will change you. Your pride, selfishness, and arrogance will be removed, and you will be filled with love for others. Your hard, resistant heart will be transformed, and you will find that your new undivided heart longs for and seeks God's will for your life.

Changed

Day 41 Exercises

1. Describe how you have been living with a divided heart.

___

2. How have you been hard-hearted?

___

3. What does life with an undivided heart look like?

___

4. How will you draw close to the Lord and allow His Spirit to transform you?

___

DAY 42
NO YOKING

> *Galatians 5:1*
>
> *"It is for freedom that Christ has set us free. Stand firm, then, and do not let yourselves be burdened again by a yoke of slavery."*

Today's verse reminds us that it is God's desire for us to be free. The truth is God desires so much for us to be free that He sent Christ to ensure our freedom. God, through Christ, canceled our debt, pardoned our guilt, and revoked all charges. God Himself canceled every accusation that stands against us. Our sins are forgiven through Christ, and God remembers them no more.

As we contemplate this truth, let me pose a question: If God desires for us to be free, and we want to be free, then why are so many still held captive? The answer to this question may be hard to accept, but according to Scripture, so many remain bound by sin because they choose to be. I know this answer will not be popular, and many will try to argue, but God does not lie, and His Word is clear. It is our choice to stand firm or not. It is our choice to allow ourselves to be "burdened again" or to walk in freedom.

If we had no choice, then God wouldn't have told us not to let ourselves be burdened again by the yoke of slavery. If we are ever going to overcome addiction or any other form of sin, we must come to grips with the truth that we have a choice. The enemy would have us believe we have no control, no choice, and no ability to change our behaviors. The devil wants us to agree with him that change is impossible or at least improbable. He will use any and every tactic to highlight our failures and diminish our successes. He knows that the battle is in the mind. If we believe we can't stop actively participating in the sins that bind us, then we will remain forever captive to them.

Our failure to believe God's Word and our lack of understanding of the work of Christ on the cross is all it takes to keep us trapped. Psychologists state that individuals cannot live in a manner they do not view themselves in. In other words, if I believe I am a failure, then I will live a life that fulfills my beliefs. If I view myself as an addict, then I will remain addicted. The list could go on forever. Within these same confines, if I believe that God has set me free, that he has delivered me from my sins, and that they no longer bind me, then I will live my life according to what I believe, free.

The battle for freedom begins and ends in our thoughts. This is why Scripture tells us in 2 Corinthians 2:5, "We demolish arguments and every pretension that sets itself up against the knowledge of God, and we take captive every thought to make it obedient to Christ." We must capture our thoughts and make them obedient to Christ. When we do, we will live in victory, be overcomers, and walk in freedom. The way in which we make our thoughts "obedient to Christ" is by making sure they line up with God's Word.

We will be free when we align our thoughts and beliefs with God's Word. The written Word discredits every statement, argument, or thought that is against God's truth. All we have to do is obey, "stand firm," and not let ourselves be bound up by the things Christ has delivered us from. It really is our choice.

Changed

Day 42 Exercises

1. What sins have you been enslaved you?

2. If you are in Christ why do those sins have any authority or power over you?

3. What would keep you from being set free?

4. What thoughts keep you from standing firm on God's promises of freedom?

Week 7

> *"We need more than just a slight change, we need to be transformed,"*

We have been taking a deep look into the lies we have believed, our preconceived ideas and truth of God's design for each of us. One of the things we should be certain of is in our own power we will never be able to change who we are. Some may argue this point and while there may be some validation that many individuals adjust their behavior without Devine intervention, the truth remains that while they may participate more or less in certain behaviors they are essentially the same. The reality is only the One who designed us is able to shape and mold us into that perfect design.

In and of ourselves we end up trading one vice for another. One of the easiest example we can see is those who trade substance abuse to food abuse. While they may finally be free from the substances that controlled them and caused so much pain and problems they remain bound to another trap of enslavement that is only more socially acceptable. To be delivered, to be free, we must have God remove our shortcoming. He is the only One who can change us. This week as we move forward we need to ask God to reveal the areas where we fall short and seek to allow Him to remove those things from our lives.

As God changes and molds us, it is important we reject any previous beliefs about who we are. If we continue to see ourselves as the same old person, just trying to do better then we will always remain the same old person, with just a little more or a little less of the things we like and dislike about ourselves. We need more than just a slight change, we need to be transformed, we need to move from darkness to light, from death to life and from defeat to victory.

In God's Word we are called: complete, whole, cleansed, the righteousness of the Lord, a light, the salt of the earth, the head, friend of God, heir, a child of God, and so many great and wonderful things. This is who we are in Christ: who we are when we surrender our will to His will. When we accept Christ as our Savior, He transforms us from the kingdom of darkness to the kingdom of light. When light enters darkness, darkness ceases to be.

There literally isn't anything deficient in your life that God is not able to correct. There aren't any habits, behaviors, or attitudes that God can't set right. Arriving at this understanding is crucial in becoming that "new you." When we accept and understand these truths, then we must admit the only reason God hasn't taken our shortcomings, changed our attitudes or corrected our behaviors is because we haven't let Him. Although God could change us against our will, He won't because He has given each of us our own free will choice.

Changed

We choose to adopt the identities we have claimed. No one forced them upon us, nor did we happen to fall into them. Each and every aspect of our identity has been claimed through our own free will choice. Many would argue this point and would use addiction as an example. They would point out no one ever chooses to be an addict. It may even be true that no one wakes up thinking to themselves, "I want to be an addict." However, they certainly made their own choice to do all the things that lead to their addiction.

The same is true for walking in the freedom that Christ has provided us. It is our choice; we only simply need to believe what the Bible says about who we are in Him and what He is willing to do and has already done for us. It is absurd to think the God who created us won't fulfill His will within us. To believe God won't transform us is to believe that God would have Jesus come to earth, humble Himself to the point that He had to be cared for by His own creation, knowing that He would be rejected, persecuted and crucified for absolutely no reason.

We must get beyond the deceptions, the excuses and our own pride. God sent His Son to pay the penalty for our freedom so that we can be exactly who He created us to be: complete, whole, able and not lacking anything. The same power that raised Christ from the dead is the same power that lives in those who are His. That resurrecting, life-giving power is more than able to break our chains, remove our shortcomings and set us free. It's time to believe.

DAY 43
HE CARES

> *1 Peter 5:6-7*
>
> *"⁶ Humble yourselves, therefore, under God's mighty hand, that he may lift you up in due time. ⁷ Cast all your anxiety on him because he cares for you."*

Today's passage begins with humility. We just discussed how Christ humbled Himself to come on our behalf. In our verse today, we read that we are to humble ourselves under God's mighty hand so that He can lift us up when the time comes. It is important that we understand what it means to humble ourselves. First, we must understand humility is not to be meek, mild, or weak. In fact, being humble requires more strength and resolve than it does not to be humble. We need to understand being humble does not mean you have no ability to change the situation in which you are exhibiting humility. In reality, we can only be humble when we have authority, choice, and the ability to respond differently. In other words, it isn't humility if you don't have a choice.

Grasping what humility is, we must then seek to know what it means to humble ourselves before the "mighty hand of God." To humble ourselves under His mighty hand is to open our hearts to His Word, to put His will above our own, to stop focusing on our own desires, and to focus on fulfilling God's desires for us. It requires us to confess our sins, repent, and give our worries, fears, and concerns to the Lord, all the while being confident that He will guide, provide, and intervene according to His will. When we humble ourselves before God, it puts us in a place of trust, acceptance, and receptiveness.

Waiting is one of those things we just don't like to do. As most of us have figured out, the best things in life are well worth the wait. Unfortunately, our flesh is wired to desire instantaneous results. Our impatience is why most of us have such a hard time humbling ourselves before God and waiting for Him to lift us up in due time. Unfortunately, we want instantaneous change, instantaneous victory. We don't want to have to work for it, much less wait for it. Many of us know Isaiah 40:31 states: "Those who hope in the Lord will renew their strength. They will soar on wings like eagles; they will run and not grow weary, they will walk and not be faint. "Those who wait on the Lord shall renew."

We have this promise: if we will humble ourselves and wait on God, He will lift us up, He will empower us, and He will enable us. The rest of our verse today brings all this together with a simple reminder that we can and should cast all our fears, concerns, and anxiety on the Lord, for He cares for us (1 Peter 5:7). We are not throwing our problems at a distant, disconnected, unconcerned higher power. No, we are laying all our problems at the feet of the One and Only individual who truly cares more for us than we do for ourselves. Even better than that is the fact that He alone is the One who can intervene, correct, and deliver us from all those things that have been destroying us.

I know when I have gotten out of the way, given my problems to God, and waited on Him, I have always found victory. Let me encourage you to trust His Word, wait on God, and surrender your will to Him. In other words, humble yourself. When you do, you, too, will find the victory, freedom, and ability you need to accomplish all that God has planned for you.

Changed

Day 43 Exercises

1. List the areas in your life that are the hardest to surrender to God.

___

2. What does humbling yourself to God mean to you?

___

3. What problems, fears, cares and anxieties do you have currently that you need God's intervention?

___

4. What does waiting on God look and feel like?

___

DAY 44

> *Isaiah 64:8*
>
> *"Yet You, Lord, are our Father. We are the clay, You are the potter; we are all the work of Your hand."*

SHAPE ME

Today's verse serves as a reminder that we did not create ourselves. From a young age, we are told to be a self-made individual, to take responsibility for our lives, and that if we want something, we will have to get it for ourselves. This is in direct conflict with what Scripture teaches. God's Word declares that we are made in His image, created for a purpose, and that God specifically designed us. This means all of our original character traits, untainted by sin, are directly from God.

As we surrender to the Lord and allow Him to have His way with us, He will mold us into who He originally created us to be, and He will enable us to accomplish all that He has planned. In the beginning, God took the dust of the Earth and formed man in His image. After molding and shaping man with careful intent, God then breathed life into His creation. The very hands of God carefully shaped and constructed mankind's physical attributes, and the very breath of God gave us life.

One of the things that we must understand is that when God created all things when He constructed the universe, He did not just put everything into motion and then become a distant observer. God remained and still remains actively involved with all that He created. Today's verse serves as a reminder that just as God shaped mankind in the beginning, He is still molding and shaping us today. The free will choice He gave mankind has allowed us to make decisions that have affected our design. Sin perverts, it deteriorates, and it destroys that which it affects. Sin has infected and affected each of us. The results of our own disobedience and the disobedience of others have put us in the situation we are in now. Whether we want to admit it or not, all the struggles we face today directly result from sin entering the world. The only cure for sin is Jesus. We can't be good enough to overcome sin, we can't be Holy enough on our own, and we certainly can't pay the price to find freedom from sin. Only the Lord Jesus Christ was able to and did pay the price for sin. He alone is the only One Holy enough to meet the requirements necessary to cure sin.

When we surrender to the Lord, accept Him as our Savior, and are born again, the Lord takes up residence in us through the Holy Spirit, and then and only then have we found the cure for sin. The more we allow Him to live through us, the more we surrender to His direction, and the more we obey Him, the less sin, past, present, and future can affect who we are and what we do. In essence, we are molded by God into who He desires us to be from the inside out. Bit by bit, those attitudes and behaviors that don't belong in us are surrendered, released, and we are set free.

The breath of God is His Spirit. This means that the same power breathed life into dust and the same power that raised Christ from the dead is the same power that comes to live in you and me. When we grasp the significance of this, and we allow Him to have His way, there is no way we won't be changed, delivered, and empowered to be who He created us to be.

Changed

Day 44 Exercises

1. What has been a part of who you are that you are certain is not God's design for you?

2. Explain what it mean to have the breath of God live within you.

3. Describe your life completely surrendered and lead by God.

4. What is keeping you from allowing God to live through you?

DAY 45
GOOD NAME

> *Proverbs 22:1*
>
> *"A good name is more desirable than great riches; to be esteemed is better than silver or gold."*

What are you striving for? What are you working so diligently to achieve? Is your goal to have more money, a big house, to live comfortably? While there is nothing wrong, in and of itself, with desiring financial security and a comfortable existence. To seek those things above God and His plan for you is sin. Instead of seeking comfort or material possessions, we should strive to establish ourselves as followers of Christ who are men and women of our word. Not so long ago, the cultural belief instilled in us from birth was to keep our word. We were told things like: "All you have is your word" and "Your word should be as good as gold." We understood the importance of being honest and truthful. Commitments were kept, and we did what we said we would do. Many, even in today's generation, can relate to these teachings. Unfortunately, what was once a prized predominant social value has lost its priority as a whole in society.

The value of keeping one's word has continued to decay through every generation. Without purposeful and meaningful change, things deteriorate, not improve. In Jesus' time, society operated under a barter system, and having a good name, as our passage states today, was imperative. After all, if you were a fisherman and wanted to trade fish for olive oil, you would simply make the deal based on your word. After all, you would not likely be carrying a mess of fish in your pocket with which to trade. Your declaration to bring a mess of fish the next time you went fishing to trade for the olive oil right then and there was all that was necessary. A "good name" was essential, and keeping your word was imperative. The fact we no longer operate under a barter system does not lessen the importance of being trustworthy, fair, and honest.

Those who have a "good name" are respected, trusted, and admired even in today's culture. Those who possess this quality have no need to promise or swear. People know they will do what they say. They are known to keep their word and be true. You know they will be there when they tell you they are coming. If people make you promise or swear to believe you, then it means you are known to lie. If promises are required, then you are simply not trustworthy, and you've been dishonest or undependable in the past. The worst part is that you know it and haven't done something about it. Many who picked up this book seeking change may not have even known they needed to change this area of their lives. Most readers are seeking to change only those big destructive areas, those parts of their lives that have crippled them mentally, emotionally, and physically. While overcoming an addiction, leaving the occult, or stopping bad behaviors are all needed and seem inherently more important than having a good name, we must remember those crippling behaviors started with small, seemingly unimportant compromises. No one wakes up one day and says, "I want to be addicted to substance; I want to destroy my life, my relationships; and I want to end up alone, broke, and shunned." Each of those big areas you are seeking to change all started with something small. This is why we can't overlook those seemingly unimportant life instructions. Seeking a "good name" and living a life that gives God glory and honor brings us to the life most of us seek. Living with a good name, integrity, and trustworthiness will give you a good reputation in your community and keep you from compromises that lead to destruction. There is a saying that uses the following initials: W.W.J.D. This stands for What Would Jesus Do? The idea is to ask yourself, "Would Jesus do this, would Jesus say this, would Jesus act like this," and so forth. The truth is, if we would live according to what Jesus would do, what would honor Him and live a life that gives Him and us a good name, the change we desire would be a natural byproduct of our good choices.

Changed

Day 45 Exercises

1. What big areas are you trying to change?

2. Including the small things, what behaviors do you have that hinder you having a good name?

3. What would a God honoring, good name, life look like?

4. Share the small, seemingly unimportant, behaviors you will allow God to change in your life so that you give Him and you a good name.

DAY 46

CHOSEN

> *John 15:16*
>
> *"You did not choose Me, but I chose you and appointed you so that you might go and bear fruit, fruit that will last and so that whatever You ask in my name the Father will give you."*

Chosen means to be selected as the best and most appropriate. I know most of us can relate to being picked for some form of team sport. As kids in elementary school, the two most popular kids would square off as team captains and then choose who they wanted on their teams. Many times, I was chosen first and many times, last or next to last. Usually, those self-appointed team captains picked their best friends first. Then, they would choose those they knew were the best, most athletic, or most liked. While everyone knew someone had to be last, no one wanted to be the last two people left to choose from because that meant that nobody wanted you on their team; they were just stuck with you.

Those feelings of not being chosen, being the leftovers, or the last resort are exactly what the enemy wants us to believe we are. He knows if he can diminish the true value of who we are to God and the importance of our calling, he can render our impact ineffective and unproductive. If we would be honest with ourselves, most of us reading this book, looking for change, have been living an ineffective and unproductive life. We know we are on the team, but we have felt like the last kid waiting to be picked; who knows, they only got on the team because there was no one else to choose from. We haven't walked boldly, acted confidently, or lived in authority.

Today's verse even takes this truth of being chosen a step deeper. Beyond having believed that we were a last resort pick by God, the enemy has made many of us feel as though God never even wanted us to begin with. We have felt like He didn't choose us but that we chose Him. Believing we chose to join God's team because it was better and more desirable than all the other teams puts all the work on us. We begin to live as if we are constantly trying out, hoping and praying that we don't get cut, left behind, or traded for someone better.

The Scriptures clearly define our real worth and value as God declares we did not choose Him, but He chose us. Everything changes when we know our real worth, our true value, and how important we are to God. We aren't God's last resort but His first choice. He chose you over all those who are living right here and right now. God chose you. All of us on the team are first round draft picks. We are not at the bottom of the barrel. We are the best-suited, most able, and completely capable of accomplishing that which God has chosen us for. We are choosing to bear fruit; this means to witness, to share His love, and to live a life that brings Glory to God. We are to lead all those who are hurting, lost, and in need to the One who gave His all for them.

We are chosen to be His representatives on Earth. We are His ambassadors. God chose us to be an extension of who He is, and this is why He continues to say, "Whatever you ask in my name, the Father will give you". (John 14:15). Chosen! We are chosen to carry His very presence; and therefore, chosen to act, operate, and move on His behalf. There really isn't anything He has called us to do that we cannot accomplish through Him. Stop living as though you are just existing and live as He created you to be.

Changed

Day 46 Exercises

1. Share the results of believing you choose God instead of Him choosing you.

2. How does realizing God picked you above all others impact you?

3. What has God chosen you for?

4. What feelings should I reject and repent for accepting about my importance to God?

DAY 47
NEW NAME

> *Revelation 2:17*
>
> *"Whoever has ears, let them hear what the Spirit says to the churches. To the one who is victorious, I will give some of the hidden manna. I will also give that person a white stone with a new name written on it, known only to the one who receives it."*

Today's passage talks about "the one who is victorious." The victory spoken of here is of those who receive eternal life, to those who have been born again. "To the one who is victorious," is symbolic in the use of the word "one." The idea conveyed is the biblical truth that it is the minority not the majority who become victorious. Similar to the teaching in Matthew 7:14 "but small is the gate and narrow the road that leads to life, and only a few find it." The passage continues to communicate this same message as it speaks of receiving the "hidden manna."

For a quick reference, manna is the bread-like substance that God used to feed the nation of Israel while they were in the desert after escaping Egypt. It was flakes of food God laid out across the ground each day. This manna, which literally means, "what is this," would only last for a day before it spoiled, except on the sixth day. On that day, the nation was told to gather enough for two days so that they may observe the Sabbath day of rest. God was teaching all of us we need to be nourished daily by the Lord. It is important to note that having to gather daily also points to the fact that we can't live on what He did yesterday. We need spiritual nourishment every day. A one-time or once-a-week touch by God will never be enough to sustain us. This is why getting in His Word, studying, worshiping, and praying on a daily basis is so important.

Manna doesn't stop there. In the New Testament, Jesus declares He is the Bread that has come down from Heaven. He compares His being here to an even greater nourishment than what was given in the time of Moses, and He declares that to have eternal life, one must partake of Him as the Living Bread. This, of course, is not ingesting His physical body but a declaration that we must partake of His Spirit, His Word and His Love in our lives. Just as physical bread is ingested and all of its nourishments are carried throughout every cell of our body, He, too, must be allowed to nourish every spiritual cell of our body. The correlation of Jesus as the manna is imperative to understanding this passage. This passage states the manna is hidden. Again, this is to symbolically show not everyone will get it. The manna being hidden and only given to "the one who is victorious" means that this nourishment, the Bread of Life, is only for those who are born again. No matter what you have been told or what you may have even believed, not everyone will be pardoned, forgiven, or find eternal life in Heaven. Only those who receive the Bread of Life, those who accept Jesus as their Lord and Savior, will be victorious. Jesus' words in John 6:51 explain it best. "I am the living bread that came down from Heaven. Whoever eats this bread will live forever. This bread is My flesh, which I will give for the life of the world." (NIV)

As we continue reading today's verse, we see that born again believers are promised "a white stone with a new name written on it." The significance of the white stone is in reference to a court acquittal or a not guilty verdict. In Ancient Greece, when casting a vote of innocence, a white stone would be used, while a black stone would signify guilt. A white stone was also used in the Roman era as a ticket given to the victor of a competition. This white stone ticket gave entrance to the banquet celebration for all the winners of their competitions. We, as believers, are those who are victorious. We have been acquitted of our sins, and we will join the King at His banquet table.

Day 47 Exercises

1. What must you do to be "one who is victorious?"

2. Explain how you can partake of the Heavenly manna?

3. How are you counted as one who is acquitted and victorious in life?

4. Explain why you are still struggling as a born again believer with all that Christ has done for you?

DAY 48
GOD-ITUDE

> *Ephesians 4:22-24*
>
> *"²² You were taught, with regard to your former way of life, to put off your old self, which is being corrupted by its deceitful desires ²³ to be made new in the attitude of your minds; ²⁴ and to put on the new self, created to be like God in true righteousness and holiness."*

Before we get to the God-itude in our passage today, we should pay close attention to verse twenty-two above. It states, "to put off your old self, which is being corrupted by its deceitful desires." Pay attention to the words "put off." This is an action, a calling that we must do. No one else can do it. It is up to us. It won't happen by accident. It must be intentional.

Along with putting off the old self, we are told "to put on the new self." Again, this action is our responsibility. Wanting and waiting for our old self not to be there anymore and for our new self to suddenly show up won't just happen. We must do our part. We are to get rid of all those old habits, desires, and behaviors and put on the righteousness and holiness required.

We must develop God-itude if we are going to be victorious. God-itude is the new attitude spoken of in today's passage that behaves, acts, and is like God, Righteous and Holy. Scripture tells us in Philippians chapter four that we are able to do all things with Christ. The unspoken part of that verse means without Christ, we can do nothing right, holy or pure. Without His help, power, and direction, we will be bound to and stuck in our old ways with no hope of change. Yet we are told to do the putting off and the putting on. This is the conundrum most of us have been living in; we've been trying to do what only God can. Even worse, is doing nothing yet expecting something to change.

The answer lies in a passage of Scripture in Matthew chapter six that states, "Seek first the Kingdom of God, and His righteousness, and all these things will be added unto you." It is from seeking a deep relationship with the Lord that we find the ability to put away, put off, and overcome those old ways. Even so, it still becomes our choice whether we allow God to help us or not. Trying to change who we are in our own power will never be enough. We might be able to set aside certain behaviors for a while, but they will find their way back or be replaced by something just as bad, if not worse. Changing who we are without God is impossible. We may be able to adjust certain aspects with a little more or less of what we are working on, but nonetheless, we will still be the same.

Real change only comes from the transformation we find as we grow closer to Jesus. The more time we spend in worship, prayer, Bible study, and resting in His presence, the more we will be who He created us to be. This change won't be something we are forcing or disciplining ourselves to accomplish. The change will come as a cause and effect of a right relationship with the Lord. We will naturally set aside, "put off," those things that don't honor Him. In turn, it will also be a natural response to "put on" all of those Christ-like behaviors, those "God-itudes" we need in order to be more like Him. Then, our lives will be pure, holy, and righteous. We may still falter or battle with the flesh from time to time, but it will never be able to overcome us as long as we keep seeking Him.

Changed

Day 48 Exercises

1. What old self behaviors do you need to put off?

2. What steps do you need to take in order to put off what you listed above?

3. What God-itudes do you need to put on?

4. Explain the difficulty or ease you will encounter putting on those Christ-like behaviors above.

DAY 49
WHOSE PLAN

> *Jeremiah 29:11*
>
> *"For I know the plans I have for you," declares the Lord, "plans to prosper you and not to harm you, plans to give you hope and a future."*

We have all made plans for our lives. Some of those plans have probably worked out how we thought; others may have come nowhere close to what we imagined. Every plan we have ever made has been limited by what we know and expect. For example, I have never made plans to land on the moon. I am not an astronaut, haven't been to any space camps, nor have I studied any books on space travel. Consequently, I have no plans for space travel or lunar landing. The plans we make for our lives are always based on our experiences, knowledge, and understanding.

The same is true with God. The plans He has for us are limited to His understanding, His knowledge, and His experiences. We use three common words to describe God's abilities: omnipotent, omnipresent, and omniscient. This means that God is all-powerful (omnipotent), all-present (omnipresent), and all-knowing (omniscient). Simply put, God has no limits in ability, knowledge, or experience; He knows everything, understands everything, and can do everything.

Today's passage states that our all-knowing and all-powerful God has made plans for us. All the plans God has made for us are to help and prosper us. The word prosper here is not limited to financial matters, but instead, all matters. God will prosper us in "all that matters." Money is here today and gone tomorrow, and we are told that He will supply all our needs. So, we must look beyond just monetary matters when it comes to what God is specifying in this passage. The things that really matter are found in the things money can't buy, such as peace, joy, and love. I know I didn't have peace before giving my life to Christ. I struggled to find joy in my life. Joy was foreign to me. I often found things that temporarily made me happy, but they never lasted. When it came to love, I didn't even know what it was, which makes sense. Since Scripture states that "God is love," it would be impossible to truly know love without knowing God.

Even beyond the fact that God has plans to prosper us, today's verse continues to explain these plans are not to harm us but to give us hope and a future. This is an amazing promise from the Lord and one we can rest on. In fact, we should build upon this promise, as God cannot lie. Therefore, what He has said will come true. Many times in life while serving God in obedience, it seemed that everything was going wrong, that everyone was against me, and that God Himself had turned His back on me. Regardless of what I may have felt, the truth was that God was working for my benefit to prosper me, not to harm me, and to give me hope and a future. Knowing this has made all the difference for me. I pray you will hold on to this truth and that it makes it much easier to face life's difficulties. As a believer, we are promised the end will be better than the beginning. We have a future that is glorious and literally Heavenly.

Changed

Day 49 Exercises

1. Is it possible to limit what God can do in your life?

2. How do you feel about today's passage?

3. What are you going through that seems to go against today's verse?

4. Pray about the above situation and write what God is sharing with you about it.

Week 8

> *"All it takes to find the life that God designed for us is to live by faith that God is who He says He is and we are who He says we are."*

The issue with most of us is that we have tried so many times to become a better version of ourselves. We pick and choose the things we don't like about ourselves or the things that seem to be the most detrimental, and we try to change those things. For example, those who are overweight often try many different diets. Some of those diets work for a short period, but often, after losing the weight, somehow, it seems to be found right back with a few extra friends tagging along. The same is true for those with an addiction; people will try to stop using the substances that control them, only to find themselves relapsing or replacing that substance with another.

The truth is we don't need a fixed-up, patched-over, better version of ourselves. What we need is a total transformation. We don't just need to change those obvious life-controlling habits. We need the part of ourselves that has taken comfort in those habits to be removed and replaced by what and how God designed them to be in the first place.

We need an identity change, a new name, a new purpose, and a new understanding of who we are. We can't skip transformation if we are going to change who we are. We must reach a point where we can understand who we are in Christ. Knowing our identity is essential to finding the change we desire. Studies have shown that we, as individuals, will live out what identities we internally believe to be true about ourselves. For example, when we are called stupid, no good, and told we could never do anything right, we can either choose to reject or accept these identities as who we are. People who reject those identities spend most of their lives proving those name-callers wrong, and they are often very successful at it. Those who accept those identities as true will find they always end up projecting those identities into their lives. They end up living and behaving stupidly, never accomplishing anything to be proud of, and sabotaging their own lives.

We can define the truths above simply by understanding that there is power in a name. The grade school poem may say, "Sticks and stones may break my bones, but words will never hurt me." The "may" sounds good, but we all know those names hurt. At times, verbal and mental abuse often have a more prolonged and more detrimental effect than any physical injury. Our worth and value to God are immensely more incredible than we can think or even imagine. After all, think of what Jesus sacrificed for us so that we can be forgiven. He endured the agony and pain of the cross. The One who created all things stepped down from His throne to be born and cared for by His very creation. He did this already knowing the pain of the rejection and betrayal that would come.

Changed

The God who would do all of this has already proven how much He loves us and just how important we truly are to Him, as well as who we are in Him. The Bible declares who we are in Christ. In my book "Created, Designed by God," I share a list of 103 identities given to those who are born again. A few of those are: "child of God, friend of God, disciple, eternally secure, protected, salt of the earth, light of the world, free, reconciled, saved, born again, redeemed, heir to the throne, loved, able to do all things, overcomer and victorious." There are many, many more listed throughout the Bible, and all declare that God treasures us. The enemy uses negative beliefs and negative thoughts to defeat us in our minds, knowing that if he can get us to accept those accusations as true, we will be rendered ineffective in the Kingdom of God.

All it takes to find the life God designed for us is to live by faith, believing God is who He says He is, and we are who He says we are. To live in any other way is to deny God's true identity and our own. Will we accept reality, or will we continue to believe the enemy's lies? I know that so many reading this are thinking, "But, I'm a sinner," and that is true. We will always fall short, miss the mark and fail to live a holy and righteous life. Nevertheless, who we really are is not dependent upon our ability or even our righteousness. No, who we really are is solely dependent on the One who created and designed us, the One who gave us life, and the One who lives through us, God Himself. The best part of all this is, God is not limited, He does not sin, and He never misses the mark. Through Him, we can never fail. We simply need to believe.

DAY 50
HANDIWORK

> *Ephesians 2:10*
>
> *"For we are God's handiwork, created in Christ Jesus to do good works, which God prepared in advance for us to do."*

When it comes to finding our new identity, today's verse gets right to the heart of the matter. It declares who created us and the purpose for which we were created. We are "God's handiwork." I can't drive home this point enough. God is the One who designed us. He is the One who made each of us. He gave us our individual, unique and special qualities. We are not broken; we may have been tainted by our sins and the sins of others, but we are not worthless. God still desires us no matter how far we have fallen, what awful things we have done, or how many people we have hurt and disappointed. The old saying, "God doesn't hate the sinner but the sin," is so very true. God loves us as His own; He sees beyond the rubbish we are carrying. God simply sees the one He created, the one He loves, and the one He died for.

We are His handiwork. God is perfect and makes no mistakes. When we look in the mirror and see all that we deem wrong about us, we should take a moment and remember we are made in the image of God. He designed us uniquely and equipped us for the appointed task, those "good works" He has prepared for us to accomplish. What may at first seem to be a deficiency in who we are, may actually be the defining quality that God can use in us to complete the call. These tasks are explained as being "prepared in advance." This means that those things we are called to are not by happenstance or by accident. The fact is, God has been at the center of everything, orchestrating people, situations, and circumstances in order to prepare your task. Not only has He been working from the beginning to bring all this about, but He has been with us, leading, guiding, and intervening even without our knowledge so that we would be prepared and ready to accomplish His purpose. Even when we were in the midst of our disobedience, God was watching over us. He has been gathering our mistakes and mess since birth, patiently waiting to turn all of it and us into His masterpiece. The Bible is clear for those who love Him and are called according to His purpose: He works all things, both positive and negative, together for good. This is His promise to us, and we can trust Him. No matter how bad it has gotten, God can and will turn it all for good if we accept His call and love Him.

Let me share one of the things God revealed to me about being created perfect for the task. The first thing we must understand is the devil cannot create. Only God can create. The devil can pervert and contaminate, but he cannot create. I was created with what some would call an addictive personality; I prefer to call it an extremely committed personality. I used to think I was broken, messed up, and at times, deficient because of that character trait. When I finally understood that God created me with this character trait and it was not a defect or a mistake that needed to be removed, everything changed. Remember, only God can create, so He designed me this way, and it was for a reason. God revealed to me that those who can socially drink or use substances and easily walk away are like those in the church who attend but never really get extremely involved or committed. They can use and/or participate but never be sold out. Those who have an addictive personality are the ones who have already proven they will leave their house, family, and job for what they love. These are the ones God created to be pastors, teachers, missionaries, and evangelists. God shared with me that I didn't need to rid myself of this perceived defect, but I needed to use it for what He designed it for in the first place, to serve Him wholeheartedly with even greater zeal and fortitude than the things that once consumed me.

Changed

Day 50 Exercises

1. How do you feel about being God's handiwork considering He doesn't make mistakes?

2. List those areas you have considered to be a defect or a deficiency in your character.

3. Share how those attributes listed above could be used to serve God more effectively.

4. What works do you feel God has planned in advance for you to do?

DAY 51
CALLED OUT

> *1 Peter 2:9*
>
> *"But you are a chosen people, a royal priesthood, a holy nation, God's special possession, that you may declare the praises of him who called you out of darkness into his wonderful light."*

We have been looking at the fact that God chose us and picked us. When you think of just how many people, nationalities, and ethnicities there are worldwide, it is overwhelming to think that of all the countless people God could have chosen, He hand-picked each of us for Himself. Today's verse gives a bit more insight into what we are chosen for. He chose us to be a Royal Priesthood, a Holy Nation, God's special possession.

Each one of these chosen positions has a distinct quality and characteristic. Unlike a position on a team where each individual performs a unique task and duty, these titles belong to all of His chosen, and every attribute of these individual titles belongs to all born again believers. Carefully understanding these titles may give us more insight into who we truly are. The word royal directs us straight to the King and His Kingdom. The only way anyone could be royal is to be in the line or lineage of the King. Royalty is based on who you are related to, not your abilities. When the Scripture refers to us as a priesthood, it defines us as those whom God has set apart for His service. Those within the priesthood are the ones who have direct access to God and act in obedience as His hands, feet, and mouthpiece. When we combine the words royal and priesthood, it depicts that we are those who are an heir to the throne, God's own children whom He has set apart to commune with and to act on behalf of God Himself, the King of Kings, and the Lord of Lords. He is the One who is ultimately in charge of everything. All people and things belong to Him and are under His direct charge.

We find another compound identity and position in the title Holy Nation. Holy means to be set apart for God, and nation means a large number of people united by common lineage, heritage, language, or purpose. Plainly put, we are not alone. God has chosen you, me, and many others to be united in purpose and set apart from all other nations. As a Holy Nation, we are not to look like the other nations around us. We are to stand out, look different, and portray the character of God.

The last title given to us in today's passage calls us God's special possession. The word possession means He owns us. Remember, all born again believers have been bought and paid for with the sacrifice Jesus made on the cross. His Holy and Righteous blood paid our debt and set us free from the penalty of our sins. Since we are owned, then our life does not belong to us. Our life belongs to the One who sent His son to pay the debt. We belong to God, not ourselves. The last part I want to discuss in this title is the word "special." This declaration takes us right back to being chosen, unique, desirable, significant, distinct, and important.

We are all this and more. God transforms us and bestows His identity upon us for a purpose. This purpose is to declare, share, inform, tell, and demonstrate just how great and wonderful God is. What He has done for us He desires to do for others. As we share how God delivered us from the sin that bound us and separated us from Him, we impart hope to those who need Him to do the same for them. We have a task, a call, and a purpose: to share our testimony and lead others to Him.

Changed

Day 51 Exercises

1. How does being chosen by God make you feel?

___

2. What does being a royal priesthood mean to you?

___

3. What does being a Holy Nation and God's special possession mean to you?

___

4. What does being called by God mean to you?

___

DAY 52
BEGRUDGED

> *Matthew 5:23-24*
>
> *"²³ "Therefore, if you are offering your gift at the altar and there remember that your brother or sister has something against you, ²⁴ leave your gift there in front of the altar. First go and be reconciled to them; then come and offer your gift."*

There isn't a person alive who hasn't experienced offense at someone else's hand or been the one to offend others. Part of recovery is making amends to those we have hurt, and today's passage speaks directly about making amends. Holding grudges or separating yourself from those who love you because of past mistakes is not beneficial to your health or those who have been hurt. Of course, there are times when it is not advisable or even safe to restore relationships. In fact, in certain situations, trying to restore relationships could be detrimental. When it comes to making amends, no one should seek to restore those types of relationships.

I once read a sign that said: "Holding on to bitterness is like drinking poison and wishing that the other person dies." The Bible refers to bitterness as a root. Meaning that it grows deep and it spreads. Being bitter, having unforgiveness or holding onto resentment will never benefit you. Finding it in your heart to forgive those who, by the world's standard, don't deserve it is medicine to your soul more than theirs. In fact, allowing yourself to remain in an offended state is to allow that person or persons to maintain control over you and your life. Releasing the offense and finding forgiveness is how to set yourself free from that person's grip.

In my life, I can share my own experience with some close church friends. I found myself going through a bad situation, and it seemed that when I needed those who claimed to love me the most, they were nowhere to be found. They ignored my calls, refused to be seen with me, and even turned a cold shoulder to me. They talked about me behind my back, accused me of things I didn't do, and spread rumors about me. It got so bad that I felt as though I had nobody on my side, no one to confide in, and no one to trust. It was a time in my life I felt all alone. I felt so far away from God and my entire life seemed to be falling apart. My finances, job, home life, and family were all affected on some level.

I got mad. I began to place blame where it didn't belong, and at times, right where it did belong. I allowed the offense to take over, and I became bitter; I felt wronged and rejected, and I started to pick apart all who had been unjust to me. This bitterness was projected not just on specific individuals alone. I began to blame the church and its leadership. I said things I shouldn't have. I made accusations that were wrong, yet even if true, those things should have never been shared by me. I was trying to justify my feelings and my actions based on the wrong that was done to me. All of it was wrong.

We all know two wrongs don't make a right, and I would have been better off recognizing that a lot quicker. To make a long story short, God convicted me, I repented, and I had to ask for forgiveness from people who didn't deserve it by the world's standards. This will also be true for you. The world's ways may justify your offense. However, God says, "But if you do not forgive others their sins, your Father will not forgive your sins" (Matthew 6:15).

Changed

Day 52 Exercises

1. List those whom you know you have offended.

2. List those whom have offended you.

3. What does making amends look like to you?

4. Write a prayer asking God to help you forgive those on your list and ask Him to show you what amends are needed.

DAY 53
FRIEND OF GOD

> *John 15:15*
>
> *"I no longer call you servants, because a servant does not know his master's business. Instead, I have called you friends, for everything that I learned from my Father I have made known to you."*

Friend of God, that is who and what we are when we become His. Today's passage specifies the difference between a hired hand, an outsider, one who is not close, and an individual who is a friend. One of the key points in understanding this verse's depth is comprehending the word friend. When discussing close relationships, we usually think of friends and family. Sometimes, certain family relationships are close and personal, and there are other family members we would prefer not to be related to. We simply can't choose our family; we can choose whom we allow to be a part of our lives, but we are born into a family with no choice of our own.

Friends, unlike family, are chosen. We pick them, somehow, and for some reason, we build relationships with people who, more than likely, were complete strangers to us at one time. At times, it is unexplainable why someone becomes our friend, but generally, it is because we share common likes or dislikes. Those we choose to befriend are those we like to spend time with. The more time we spend with them, the happier we tend to be.

I believe this is why Scripture refers to us as friends in this passage. I believe the Lord is trying to impress upon us that we are a joy to Him. He longs to spend time with us and takes pleasure in being with us. This is huge when you stop and think about it. The Creator of all things, the One who has all power and all authority, wants to spend His time with us. Remember, this is His choice. He is not forced to deal with us. The Lord doesn't have to be nice to his brother or sister, so to speak, to make the Father happy. No, He desires for us to be with Him. He longs for us to consider Him important enough to set all other things aside and be in His presence. He calls us friends.

This passage also specifies that we are "no longer servants." This may cause some of us a bit of confusion as we know Paul referred to himself as a bond-servant of Christ, and this was a desirable and expected position of a believer, but here it says we are no longer servants. A servant was owned and had no rights. They were there to work off debt and had no input on how they would work it off. It was at the masters' discretion as to what they were allowed to do. They were not consulted or asked for advice, and often, they were overlooked as if they were not even there.

On the other hand, a bond-servant was one who had worked for the family and chosen to stay beyond their specified time. They loved their master, and their master loved them. They did not want to leave their masters but stay with them, and because of their relationship, they would dedicate their lives to the one they choose to serve. Paul describes himself as a bond-servant, not to specify the servant part but the dedication to serve his master. He loved Jesus so much that he only wanted to work for and serve Him. The servants we all used to be were not that of a bond servant. We had no dedication; we were just existing in the Master's world, serving ourselves. Praise be to Jesus that when we are born again, we are transformed and are no longer a servant but become His friend.

Changed

Day 53 Exercises

1. How have you been living against God as a servant?

2. What does it mean to be a friend of God?

3. What does it mean to you to know that God chose you?

4. How should you now live knowing you are His friend and no longer a servant?

DAY 54
CHILD OF GOD

> *Galatians 4:6-7*
>
> *"⁶ Because you are his sons, God sent the Spirit of his Son into our hearts, the Spirit who calls out, "Abba, Father." ⁷ So you are no longer a slave, but God's child; and since you are his child, God has made you also an heir."*

We sing it, say it, and claim it, "I am a child of God," but do we know what it means to be His child? Today's verse declares we are no longer slaves but instead His very own children and heirs to God Himself. If we are to begin to grasp what this means for us, we must first understand the position of an enslaved person. To be a slave is not a circumstance or situation we are placed in but rather a position in which we remain with no thought, ability, or authority to change. A slave is owned by his or her master; a slave cannot decide what he or she wants for his or herself, nor are his or her wants or desires even considered. A slave serves his or her master whether he or she wants to or not, for it is the master who controls him or her.

Living in a culture that has rejected slavery and any form of caste system, it can be hard to fathom individuals surrendering themselves to be owned and controlled by another. While foreign to us, many other cultures still practice forms of slavery today, and in Jesus' time, it was common for one to sell his or herself into slavery to pay a debt. In Biblical times, it would be common for an individual to openly choose to remain a slave once their debt had been paid. We discussed this yesterday. These slaves would be referred to as "bondservants," and they would pierce their ears with a spike to identify their choice to remain a slave.

Many of those who remained slaves did so because they had become "like" part of the family. They were safe, loved their masters, and were treated well. The truth remained that regardless of how much the master may care for them, they were still property, could own nothing, have no money, never choose their spouse, and never have an inheritance to give any children they may have. On the other side of this relationship was the master, who owned everything and could freely choose for themselves and their slaves. The masters owned everything, and all they owned became part of the inheritance they would leave their children.

The child of the master did not have to do anything to earn the inheritance other than be born to or adopted by the master. Their abilities or character had no bearing on their position as an heir. They simply were an heir because of who they were, not what they could do. This truth should begin to set you free from needing to perform to be accepted by God. Honestly, none of us could perform well enough, right enough, or holy enough to earn a position as His children and heirs. Thankfully, we don't have to. All we have to do is receive His Spirit into our hearts and become His children.

As His child, we have His authority to accomplish all that the Father desires. Being born again into the family of God and receiving His Spirit within us enables us to live free and in the confidence of knowing who we are. We are His children. He chose us, which means all that is available to God Himself is available to us through Him. We can confidently declare, "My Daddy will take care of this," and we can confidently know it is true. We have nothing to fear because we are children and heirs to the One who owns it all, created it all, and is over all.

Changed

Day 54 Exercises

1. Describe the difference between a slave and an heir?

2. What does it mean for you that as a believer, you are a child of God?

3. Describe what your life can look like living in the confidence of being His child and heir?

4. What could hinder you from achieving what you described above?

DAY 55
MAJESTIC

> *Jeremiah 1:5*
>
> *"Before I formed you in the womb I knew you, before you were born I set you apart; I appointed you as a prophet to the nations."*

The enemy would have us believe we are the sum of our mistakes, that who we are is a result of the things we have been through and our choices. While we all deal with the consequences of everyone's free will choice, ours included, who we are is not defined by them. Our passage today clearly explains we are designed by the Lord for the Lord's purpose. The reason most of us seem to be so lost and unfulfilled is that we haven't stepped into the purpose for which He created us.

Years ago, on my way to work, I saw a bald eagle on the side of the road eating a deer that had been hit by a car. I initially thought seeing an eagle eating like a vulture was strange, but I didn't give it much thought. The next day, right there in the same spot, I saw what seemed to be that same eagle eating that same dead deer. I became more intrigued and curious about why this majestic bird behaved like a common buzzard. This happened for three days in a row, at which point I began to believe God was trying to get my attention somehow. As I contemplated these events, the Lord began to explain to me He created that eagle. He had given it all the abilities it needed. He reminded me the eagle was designed to soar high in the sky and that He had given the eagle keen eyesight to see fish swimming in the ocean from great heights. He had equipped him with large, powerful claws to pull fresh food straight out of the ocean.

I asked the Lord why this most majestic bird, the symbol of our country, with all its abilities, was eating three-day-old rotting road kill instead of the fresh food it should be. The Lord explained that the eagle had ventured away from what it was designed to do because it thought this was an easy meal with no work involved. The eagle was free to choose to live the way God designed it to or take what seemed to be the easy way out. The Lord reminded me that easy isn't always better and that compromising will always take you further and further away from your calling and purpose. The Lord quickened in my heart that this eagle had been eating dead decaying carcasses for so long that it didn't even know what it was missing. Until the eagle made a choice to be who God had created it to be, the eagle would never be at peace and never find joy.

The Lord reminded me that we humans are the most majestic beings that He has ever created. We are His crowning jewel. He designed us to soar high above this troubled world and has given us all the abilities needed to be exactly who He designed us to be. Just like that eagle, until we stop taking what seems to be the easy way out and stop doing things our way, we will always be stuck with the rotten and decaying things the world wants to give us.

He formed us not to live like we have been but to rise above. He set us apart and appointed us not to follow along but to lead. He designed us with a purpose and a plan, and this purpose and plan were set long before our parents even thought of us. He knows us, and only when we decide to surrender to His will and live according to His plan will we ever step into the freedom He has given us.

Changed

Day 55 Exercises

1. What past mistakes have you committed that have limited your current lifestyle?

_____
_____
_____
_____
_____
_____
_____
_____

2. How do you relate to the eagle in this story?

_____
_____
_____
_____
_____
_____
_____
_____

3. How does it impact you knowing God has designed and equipped you for His plan?

_____
_____
_____
_____
_____
_____
_____
_____

4. What current easy ways do you need to reject in order to step into what God has designed for you?

_____
_____
_____
_____
_____
_____
_____
_____

DAY 56
GIVING BACK

> *Luke 19:8*
>
> *"But Zacchaeus stood up and said to the Lord, "Look, Lord! Here and now I give half of my possessions to the poor, and if I have cheated anybody out of anything, I will pay back four times the amount."*

We spoke a few days ago about making amends to those we have hurt and forgiving those who have hurt us. Today's passage takes this a step further. Zacchaeus was a tax collector, and in the times of Christ, tax collectors were notorious for taking more than they were supposed to. These extra funds would go into their pockets, and because of this, they were despised. Zacchaeus was considered the worst of the worst as he was the chief tax collector. He was viewed as a traitor, a thief, and corrupt.

When Zacchaeus met Jesus, He was transformed. The moment he was born again, this transformation began. This is where our passage today comes from. As soon as he accepted Christ as being the Messiah and committed his life to him, Zacchaeus knew that he could steal no more, cheat no more and that he had to give back all he had illegally taken.

Our passage explains that because Zacchaeus was changed, he vowed to pay back four times the amount of anything he had cheated anyone out of. This is what we mean when we say a saved life is a changed life. Zacchaeus could no longer stay the same after meeting the Lord Jesus and being transformed; he had to behave differently and wanted to make up for the wrongs he had done. The idea of remaining a cheat or even changing his ways but not making it right was unfathomable to him. Even before committing to make things right with anyone wronged, Zacchaeus vowed to give half of all he owned to the poor. An unchanged tax collector could not and would not give half of his possessions to the poor or even think about paying back what he had stolen, especially paying it back four times over.

This change, making amends, paying back, and no longer doing the same things you have always done, is our real lesson today. There simply is no way to live the same way you always have once you are born again. Second Corinthians 5:17 states: "Therefore if any man be in Christ, he is a new creature: old things are passed away; behold, all things are become new." This total transformation happened for Zacchaeus, and it happened for me as well. In fact, when you examine those in the New Testament like Peter, John, Thomas, and the other disciples, they were forever changed once they met Jesus face to face. Even after Christ ascended, Saul, whom we know as Paul, encountered Jesus on the road to Damascus, and he, too, was forever changed.

This change is a natural cause and effect of knowing Jesus. It is not something we muster up in our own strength, nor is it even within our own ability to make it happen. This transforming work is done by the power of the Holy Spirit out of having a right relationship with God. All of this is a great warning for those who profess to know Jesus as their personal Savior but still remain stuck in old habits, behaviors, and ways. It is simply impossible to get right with God and remain the same.

Changed

Day 56 Exercises

1. Who have I wronged and how have I wronged them?

_____

2. What old things in my life need to be changed by the power of the Holy Spirit?

_____

3. What do you think about the cause and effect change of a right relationship with God?

_____

4. What do you need to pay back fourfold? How can you pay God back fourfold?

_____

Week 9

> *"Ask yourself: are you are defined by what you do or is what you do defined by who you are."*

In preparation for this week's studies, we are going to be taking a hard look at who we are. How would you answer if you were asked by someone, "Who are you?" Most people jump right to what they do. To give you an example, a person might say, "My name is Bob, and I am an electrician." While all of this may be true, that only tells us his name and occupation. If he were to change his name to Billy and start working as a carpenter, would he still be the same person? Of course, he would. This is why we are not our names or occupations. Who we are comes from something deeper than a name, degree, or occupation. We are God's creation; He designs us, and He defines us. Who we truly are can only be found in Him.

In God's original design for us, we are complete, whole, and lacking nothing. Due to the inception of sin, we are born with a void within that must be reconciled to God. It isn't until we surrender to Christ and accept the Lord as our Savior that we are filled with His Spirit. Only in this born-again state can we find who we are: a child of God, the righteousness of Christ, not lacking anything, victorious, free, forgiven, loved, chosen, and so much more. The reason we have lived so confused, longing to find purpose, and have seemed so lost is that we have been searching for what was missing: God Himself.

Scripture states the old self is passed away and we are made into new beings. Grasping our old identity, the one stuck in sin, the one that is self-seeking and self-centered, is no longer the driving force of who we are is the easy part. Walking out our new God-given identity is much harder because we tend to see the worst part of who we have been. We get stuck remembering all the wrongs we have done and all the mistakes we have made. The enemy himself is called the "accuser of the brethren." As the accuser, he constantly reminds us of who we used to be and the things we used to do. This makes it difficult to believe God can forget who we have been and that He can no longer remember our offenses. This idea is foreign and unfathomable to us. If we are going to live in accordance with our God-given design, it is essential we realize that Christ's sacrifice on the Cross is enough to cover every sin we have committed or ever will commit.

Since understanding our born-again identity is vital in living the victorious life God planned for us, we should place extreme importance on learning who God declares us to be. We can find these identities throughout the Scriptures, both Old and New Testaments. Through study and prayer, the Holy Spirit will reveal them to us as we meditate on His Word. Psychiatrists teach that individuals cannot live in a manner they do not deem themselves to be. This is based on Biblical teachings such as: you can do all things through Christ (Phil. 4:13), the Lord establishes our steps (Prov. 16:9), and commit ourselves to God (Psalm 37:5), trust Him (Prov. 3:5-6), and He will act on our behalf (Isa. 64:4).

Changed

Plainly put, if you believe yourself to be a failure, a loser, and unable to accomplish a task, then you won't be able to do it. On the other hand, if you believe you can accomplish the task because God will help you and you have faith that the Lord will set you free, then you will live free with God's help. We simply need to believe.

Letting God have His way with our lives is the most freeing thing we can do. Having surrendered to His will means we don't have to figure everything out. It also releases us from the responsibility of finding and achieving success in our endeavors. The outcome of our obedience rests solely in the Lord's hands. He is the One who works all things together in accordance with His plans and His desires. Since His ways are so much greater than ours and His abilities are endless, we know everything will be just as it should be. Again, in His hands, we are not only set free from sin and its consequences but we are free from the responsibility of trying to maintain control over the things out of our control and free from having to know what the results of our actions will be.

DAY 57
COMPLETE

> *James 1:2-4*
>
> *"² Consider it pure joy, my brothers and sisters, whenever you face trials of many kinds, ³ because you know that the testing of your faith produces perseverance. ⁴ Let perseverance finish its work so that you may be mature and complete, not lacking anything."*

There is a saying, "the things that don't kill us make us stronger." This statement has a foundation in today's passage. The things we go through shape, teach and guide us. At times, we may go through things that make us know we never want to do them again, and there are other experiences that are so enjoyable we try to recreate them in any way we can. Almost all of us would prefer not to endure suffering, persecution, or hardship, yet we know these things are what shape who we are. It is easy to declare God's goodness and share our faith when everything is going our way, we have everything we think we need, and it seems everything is moving in the right direction,

It is really when everything is falling apart, when we feel all alone, and it seems that no one cares, that we see what kind of believer we truly are. Today's passage states that we must accept all those trials and tribulations with pure joy. If we think that means we are supposed to be happy or grateful we have lost a loved one, been let go from a job, received a bad medical diagnosis, or stubbed our toe, this verse will never make any sense. This passage doesn't say we need to be happy, grateful, or even joyful that these things have happened. No! It is saying we should be joyful, grateful, and content that through these things, we have been given a chance to test our faith.

In other words, if you run back to the things of this world, sinful relationships, sinful habits, or even your old sinful, stinking thinking when you face these various trials, you can know that your faith is weak and needs work. If the first thing you want to do is cuss, give up, or fight back when persecuted, then you can know that you are not trusting God to handle the situation. In fact, anytime we try to fix it by our own thinking, we simply show ourselves and everyone else that we are in control of our lives, not God.

The verse goes on to talk about the testing of our faith producing perseverance. Let me share with you that only those who are stubborn for the right reasons, those who can persevere through trials and tribulation, will make it to the final reward reserved for those who believe. It takes faith to persevere, and only those who truly believe can rest in the faith necessary to overcome. The passage continues to share that through persevering faith, we become complete and mature believers who lack nothing. When we reach that level of faith in God, we will be able to face any and everything the world, the flesh, or the enemy may toss our way, knowing that we are never lacking and will always overcome.

Keep the faith, stand firm, and rest in the knowledge that every bad experience, mistake, attack, and accusation you have or will endure is an opportunity for God to shine through you. When we face these trials to bring God glory and to be used by Him in accordance with His plan, we will not only overcome the trial, but we will be one step closer to fulfilling God's plan for our lives.

Changed

Day 57 Exercises

1. What current trials or tribulations are you facing?

___

2. How should you address each of these trials?

___

3. What do the results of handling trials through faith in God look like?

___

4. How will you handle future trials, tribulations and disappointments?

___

DAY 58

WORSHIP

> *Romans 12:1-2*
>
> *"¹ Therefore, I urge you, brothers and sisters, in view of God's mercy, to offer your bodies as a living sacrifice, holy and pleasing to God this is your true and proper worship. ² Do not conform to the pattern of this world, but be transformed by the renewing of your mind. Then you will be able to test and approve what God's will is his good, pleasing and perfect will."*

Worship means different things to different people. To some, Worship is a service that includes music and preaching. To others, it is a time of singing to God, individually or corporately. You may define it as a time of intimacy with the Lord. The dictionary defines Worship as special adoration or reference shown to a Spiritual being. Our passage today states that true and proper Worship is to offer ourselves as a living sacrifice to God in a holy and pleasing way. Today's first key part of our passage comes from the portion that states we are to be a "living sacrifice." We know to sacrifice means we have to give up something, which is usually something we desire or feel we need. It wouldn't be a sacrifice if it weren't hard to let go of it. When this passage talks about being a "living sacrifice," it is not telling us to give our lives on some form of physical altar and end our physical lives. "Living sacrifice" means God wants us to live, flourish, succeed, and enjoy what He has given us. The sacrifice comes from denying our fleshly desires and choosing to live in accordance to His Word.

The second key portion of this passage comes from the statement about offering our bodies. Again, this is not a physical sacrifice. This is choosing to use who we are for His Glory. Giving our bodies means all of us; God is not looking for us to compartmentalize our lives, offering Him parts of ourselves. Instead, He wants all of us, the good, bad, and the ugly parts, too. When we give Him all of us, we are meeting the bare minimum expectation. This passage states: "Offer your bodies as a living sacrifice, holy and pleasing to God this is your true and proper worship." This means anything less is not true, not proper, and not pleasing to God. This should really help us put our lives into perspective. We often give portions of our lives over to God but hang onto other parts. It might be certain relationships, our jobs, our hobbies, or even our habits. When we hang on to parts of our lives, choosing to do what we want instead of being obedient, we are setting ourselves up for failure and are not honoring God.

Today's passage clarifies it for us when it states: "Do not conform to the pattern of this world." This means that it doesn't matter if the world accepts it or not. If God's Word or His Spirit says no, then it is wrong. We are told to be transformed by the renewing of our minds. This transformation can only come from His presence in us. He is the only One that can change our thinking and our desires. The more we rest in His presence, read His Word, study, and Worship, the more He lives in and through us and the more we are transformed. When we speak His love language, then and only then can we know what His true and perfect will is for our lives.

In case you are wondering what love language God speaks, it is obedience. This consists of obedience to His call, obedience to His Word, and obedience to His leadership. The Scripture states obedience is better than sacrifice (1 Sam. 15:22), and it is through obedience we can offer our bodies as the holy and pleasing living sacrifice we are told to be.

Changed

Day 58 Exercises

1. What do you need to sacrifice in order to honor the Lord?

2. What does it mean to you to offer your body as a living sacrifice?

3. How have you been disobedient to God in the past?

4. What would your life look like if you were speaking God's love language of obedience?

DAY 59
WHOSE BATTLE IS IT

> *2 Chronicles 20:15*
>
> *"He said: "Listen, King Jehoshaphat and all who live in Judah and Jerusalem! This is what the Lord says to you: 'Do not be afraid or discouraged because of this vast army. For the battle is not yours, but God's."*

Whose battle is it? This is where we mess it up most of the time. From a young age, we are taught to take care of number one; if we don't take care of ourselves, nobody else will, and it is up to us to make it happen. This type of independent, prideful thinking brought forth sin in the first place. To really understand the lesson in today's passage, we must go back to the beginning, the very beginning of creation. We must understand who created us and why we were created.

The answer to the first question, "Who created us," is easy: God created us. The book of Genesis shares this in detail. The answer to the second question, "Why we were created," takes us on a bit of a journey through the Scriptures. In Genesis, we are told God gave mankind dominion over all the Earth. At creation, before sin entered the Earth, when all things were just as God designed, Adam and Eve walked and talked with God. They had a personal relationship with God. This gives us some initial understanding as to why we were created.

First, we were created to have a relationship with God; He designed us to know Him. Second, God gave mankind rule or management over the rest of His creation. In our original design, the closeness of fellowship and relationship with God empower us to rule the Earth in connection with God. When sin entered the world, this relationship became broken, and so did our ability to manage the world that He created. God knew the only way for us to get back to His design for us would be for Him to make a way for us to be reconciled back to Him. This is exactly why Jesus came and paid the penalty for our sins.

When reconciled to God through being born again, we are brought back to our purpose: to have a relationship with God and have dominion over all creation. Once restored, we are no longer responsible for ourselves. We are His, complete, renewed, and not lacking, because His Spirit lives in and through us. His Spirit guides us, and He will protect and provide so we can do that which He has called us to do.

This brings us back to today's passage which states, "The battle is not yours, but God's." Restored and reconciled, we now face nothing alone. We now face every battle, every enemy, and every accusation, as one who has the Spirit of God living in and through us. When David faced Goliath, he understood the truth of the battle. The battle was not his but the Lord's. When we rest on this truth, we come to understand there is nothing we can't overcome. God cannot and will not lose. This means that we cannot and will not lose.

Resting in this truth allows us to stand on another foundational Scripture we have already addressed. Philippians 4:13: "I can do all things through Christ who strengthens me." All things include all battles over habitual sin, relationships, abilities, spiritual attacks, and anything else that comes our way. It all belongs to God, and He is victorious over all.

Changed

Day 59 Exercises

1. What battles am I currently fighting?

2. How can I stop fighting the battles in my own strength?

3. What changes in my life will be present if I truly believe the battle belongs to God?

4. Share Scriptures, other than those mentioned, that confirm God's commitment to provide for and protect those who accept Him.

DAY 60
SELFLESSNESS

> *Philippians 2:4*
>
> *"not looking to your own interests but each of you to the interests of the others."*

If there is one attribute that is exemplified throughout the Gospels, it is selflessness. Today's passage reminds us the world does not revolve around us. Everything is not supposed to be about what we want, need, or think. In fact, we are told to look after the interests of others. Caring more for others than self is love, and this is exactly what God demonstrated for us. When He sent Christ to die for us, He taught us how to love others and put their needs above our own.

Another passage of Scripture states, "Greater love has no one than this: to lay down one's life for one's friends" (John 15:13). Jesus laid down His life for each of us, and that is His expectation for His followers. We should be willing and ready to do whatever we must to help those in need, guide the lost, and share His love. When we, as believers, stop putting our wants and desires above God's guidance and other's needs, we will be able to share the Gospel message the way we were designed.

When we reach the end of our lives, the things matter to us and that we take pleasure in will be what we have done for others and what we have accomplished for God. I can't imagine facing the end of this physical life and thinking about the car I wanted to buy, the jewelry I didn't purchase, or the food I never tasted. As important as those things may seem right now, they lose their position in priorities when facing eternity. The things that will be on most of our minds will be the relationships we are leaving, the family we wonder if we will see again and if we are personally prepared to stand before our Savior.

Living a life is obedient to God and filled with His presence produces the fruit of the Spirit. The fruit of the Spirit is "love, joy, peace, forbearance, kindness, goodness, faithfulness, gentleness and self-control" (Gal. 5:22-23). My goal in life is to walk in such a manner that I not only glorify God in all my actions but to face eternity full of peace, joy, and love. I can only do this by keeping His commands, which are based on His love for each of us. This is why today's verse is so important to apply in our lives. Caring more for others than oneself is only produced by love.

The most contentment I have ever had in my personal life has not been when I was running the rat race of life, trying to keep up with everyone. Trying to have the best of everything, owning the biggest TV, the fastest car, or even having the latest gadgets never brought satisfaction, no matter what the commercials said. What has brought me the most contentment in life never comes from stuff but from knowing God has used me to help others physically, emotionally, and spiritually. My prayer for you is that you will be able to apply today's verse throughout every area of your life and that you will find the contentment, joy, and peace that come from being right where God wants you: loving, helping and serving others.

Changed

Day 60 Exercises

1. Explain ways in which you have been living selfishly.

___

2. What are ways you can look after the interest of others?

___

3. Describe the things that bring you joy and contentment.

___

4. What would your life look like if you put others' interest and needs above your own?

___

DAY 61

LOVE

> *1 John 4:20*
>
> *"Whoever claims to love God yet hates a brother or sister is a liar. For whoever does not love their brother and sister, whom they have seen, cannot love God, whom they have not seen."*

Yesterday, we came to understand the importance of putting others above self. We examined how our God did exactly that and demonstrated how to love. Today, we pick up with this same thought in our passage: the fact that we must love others. Today, we learn that holding onto hatred and bitterness against another human being is, in effect, showing we do not love God. God's love for each of us is so great that He is determined to make sure we understand it is impossible to actually love Him if we cannot love those whom He created.

Let me break this down for you just a bit. The quickest way for me to have something against you, some reason to not want to be around you, or for me to simply not like you is for you to do something against one of my children. I am sure most of you reading this will agree with me: simply mess with my kid, well then you're messing with me. I feel that today's passage is basically saying the same thing. God created each of us, and to take issue with His creation is to take issue with Him. The Scripture states in 1 John 3:15, "Anyone who hates a brother or sister is a murderer, and you know that no murderer has eternal life residing in him." This is how important it is to God that we care for one another. There will always be people that we come in contact with who are difficult to be around and may be hard to love. When life has put difficult people in my path, I always try to remember God loved these people so much He sent His very own Son to pay the penalty for them; if God loves them this much, then who am I to judge them?

I am not naïve. People in this world have done wicked things. We are not called to love the acts of sin and disobedience committed upon others. It is difficult to separate the individual from the offense, but if we are going to grow in our relationship with the Lord, we will need to find a way to release any hatred or bitterness we have been carrying. The Lord's Prayer states in Matthew chapter 6:9-13 "This is how you should pray: "'Our Father in Heaven, hallowed be your name, your Kingdom come, Your will be done, on earth as it is in Heaven. Give us today our daily bread. And forgive us our debts, as we also have forgiven our debtors. And lead us not into temptation, but deliver us from the evil one." Then, it is quickly followed by verses 14-15: "For if you forgive other people when they sin against you, your Heavenly Father will also forgive you. But if you do not forgive others their sins, your Father will not forgive your sins."

Releasing hatred and bitterness is more about your release and becoming who God has designed you to be than it is about releasing the individual that hurt you to be who God created them to be. We are not responsible for what they do with any forgiveness we extend them. It is their choice to receive it and allow it to improve their lives, or they may choose to stay the same as they have always been. Again, the outcome of extending forgiveness is not our responsibility. What is certain is that we will be different and more like Christ, and our relationship with God will not be hindered. In forgiving others and releasing hatred or bitterness, God does not expect us to put ourselves in harm's way or allow ourselves to be abused or taken advantage of. At times, forgiving is done from a distance within yourself, far from harm's way. God will guide you in how He desires you to love Him in regard to others.

Changed

Day 61 Exercises

1. Write a list of those whom you have found it hard to love or forgive.

2. Describe what your bitterness has brought you or share any benefit you have gotten from it.

3. How does knowing Jesus died for those listed in question one effect how you feel about them?

4. Share what you think God is leading you to do about your relationships with those listed above.

DAY 62

SQUEEZED

> *2 Corinthians 4:8-9*
>
> *"⁸ We are hard pressed on every side, but not crushed; perplexed, but not in despair;" ⁹ persecuted, but not abandoned; struck down, but not destroyed."*

Today's passage states: "We are hard pressed on every side, but not crushed; perplexed, but not in despair; persecuted, but not abandoned; struck down, but not destroyed." These verses speak about the struggles and trials we face as believers. We all know life can be challenging. There are times when what we are going through may even seem unbearable. However, today's verse reminds us that God understands what we face. He promises that even when we are being hit from every side, we are not alone. He is with us. Our passage today is God's reminder that He has all the power and ability necessary to sustain us when we are going through difficult times.

As followers of Christ, we are not immune to the challenges and struggles of life. Jesus Himself said that in this world, we will have trouble (John 16:33). As believers, we have the hope and promise of eternal life with God. We have the promise of abundant life, not only in the eternal life that is to come but in the one we are in right now. Knowing this should help sustain us even in the darkest of times.

The first part of our passage says, "We are hard pressed on every side, but not crushed." The imagery used of being hard-pressed on every side is powerful. It conveys a sense of being surrounded by difficulties from every side and feeling like there is no way out. However, our promise from God, in this verse, reminds us we won't be crushed no matter what. We may feel pressed, but we are not defeated because the strength of God lives within us. We are always able to draw from His power, which can persevere through any trial. The second part of the verse says, "perplexed, but not in despair." When we face difficult situations, it can be easy to feel overwhelmed and uncertain. We may not know what to do or where to turn. But even in these moments, we can find hope in Christ. We can trust God is with us and that He has a plan for our lives. We may not understand everything happening, but we can have faith that God is working all things together for our good (Romans 8:28).

The third part of the verse says, "persecuted, but not abandoned." Christians throughout history have faced persecution for their faith. Even today, there are many places in the world where believers are persecuted and even killed for following Jesus. Despite this, our passage today reminds us that in the midst of persecution, we are not abandoned. God is always with us, and He promises to never leave us nor forsake us (Hebrews 13:5). The final part of the verse says, "struck down, but not destroyed." This is perhaps the most powerful part of the verse. It speaks to the fact that when we feel as though we may have been knocked down, beaten up, and overrun by what life has brought our way, we are not destroyed. We may face setbacks, but we are not defeated. This is because we have the power of God within us. His strength can help us rise again, even when we feel we have been completely defeated.

As we hold onto this verse, we can find hope and encouragement in the midst of our struggles. Remember, no matter what we face, we are not alone. We have the power of God within us to help us persevere through any trial. We can draw on His strength and trust in His goodness, knowing that He is working all things together for our good. May this passage be a pillar of hope and strength as we navigate the challenges of life, and may we always remember our God is with us now and forever.

Changed

Day 62 Exercises

1. Describe how life has overwhelmed you and tried to break you.

___

2. How do you feel about the promises God has made to you in 2 Corinthians 4:8-9?

___

3. Describe your life free from despair.

___

4. What will change about your life based on the truth of this passage?

___

DAY 63
DON'T GIVE UP

> *Galatians 6:9*
>
> *"Let us not become weary in doing good, for at the proper time we will reap a harvest if we do not give up."*

Today's verse is a reminder for us as believers not to give up doing what God has called us to do. Life is full of challenges and trials that can often leave us feeling drained and exhausted. It's easy to become discouraged and feel like giving up, especially when it feels like you are doing everything you can to be obedient to the Lord, and you seem to be going nowhere. However, as Christians, we are called to persevere and keep doing good even when it seems our efforts are not producing results.

Paul is encouraging us in today's passage to continue in our faith and not give up on doing what is right. He reminds us there will come a time when we will reap a harvest for our efforts, but we must not lose heart in the meantime.

As believers, we are called to walk in righteousness and to do good works that bring glory to God. These good works are rooted in the "fruit of the Spirit," love, joy, peace, patience, kindness, goodness, faithfulness, gentleness, and self-control (Gal. 5:22-23). However, it's important to note that these good works are not done in order to earn our salvation but rather as a response to the grace and love that God has already shown us. In our journey of faith, it's easy to become weary and discouraged when we don't see immediate results from our efforts. We may be tempted to give up or to become complacent in our walk with God. However, this verse reminds us that if we persevere and continue to do good, we will eventually reap a harvest.

This harvest can come in many different forms. It may be a spiritual breakthrough, a restored relationship, or a tangible blessing we have prayed for. Whatever form it takes, the harvest is a reminder that God is faithful and our efforts are not in vain. In addition to encouraging us to persevere, this verse also reminds us to trust in God's timing. The harvest will come "at the proper time," which means it may not happen according to our timeline or expectations. However, we can trust that God knows what is best for us and that He will bring about the harvest in His perfect timing.

This verse also reminds us of the importance of community. The "us" in this verse refers to the body of believers, and it's clear that Paul is not speaking to individuals in isolation. As Christians, we are called to support and encourage one another in our journey of faith. We can lean on our brothers and sisters in Christ when we feel weary and discouraged, and they can do the same with us.

Our passage today is a powerful reminder to keep pressing on regardless of what things may look like at the moment. Our promise is, if we persevere and continue, we will see God move, and we will see a harvest. This harvest may not come according to our timeline or expectations, but we can trust that God knows what is best for us and that He will bring it about in His perfect timing. Furthermore, as we continue serving the Lord, we can lean on our brothers and sisters in Christ for support and encouragement, knowing that we are not alone in our struggles. Stand firm, keep our eyes fixed on Jesus, the Author and Perfecter of our faith, who has promised to be with us every step of the way.

Changed

Day 63 Exercises

1. What good works do you feel God is calling you to?

2. What might you face that could cause you to grow weary in your good works?

3. What does reaping a harvest mean to you?

4. How can you be a help to your family in Christ to help them not grow weary?

Week 10

"When you know who you are, you know what to do"

We all have years of experience doing things our way. Unfortunately, our way doesn't really work. If it did, then you wouldn't be looking to find a new and better you in Christ. When looking at the steps of recovery, the fourth step is considered one of the most challenging and pivotal points to work through. For those unfamiliar, the fourth step is to make a searching and fearless moral inventory of ourselves. You can see where this is difficult as it causes us to look at all those hurtful things we have done as well as examine our motives behind all that we do.

Reaching your true identity requires you to address all of those fears which have held you back, as well as to acknowledge your mistakes and take ownership of your actions. There really is no one else to blame but yourself for who you are and what you've done with your life. Recognizing it all rests squarely on you, not your parents, spouse, or siblings, is crucial to finding victory. The enemy desires us to place blame everywhere but where it actually belongs. If he can get you to blame someone else or get you to believe that all of this was out of your control, then you will never take the steps necessary to find the life that Christ designed for you.

Let me explain: Many people like to blame their parents for raising them wrong, putting them in bad situations that caused them to endure abuse, or for being absent, uncaring, or less than nurturing. They use their parents' failures as an excuse for their failures, often perpetuating the same cycles of neglect and abuse. This constant blame game shifts responsibility from themselves to the one that caused them the pain that they believe crippled them.

While it may be true that they endured horrific situations and they may really have suffered trauma by no choice of their own, they are still responsible for how they continue to respond to what took place. When one learns that they don't have to continue to be a victim but can choose to be victorious, this is when healing comes. We are responsible for our choices, not the choices of others, and when others' choices affect us, we are then only responsible for how we respond.

Taking responsibility for ourselves opens the door for healing and reconciliation. Part of reconciliation is forgiveness; often, the hardest person to forgive is ourselves. Again, the enemy desires us to be stuck holding onto bitterness towards those who have hurt us and towards ourselves for our failures. Just like he tempted Eve to sin, and when she did, he condemned her for it, he is doing the same thing today with us, tempting and then condemning. God knows this, and just as He provided a way out for Adam and Eve, He provided a way out for us.

His way out for us is Jesus. God knew we couldn't do it on our own, so He sent His Son to pay our debt and set us free. When we accept Christ as our Lord and Savior, we are no longer bound by our sins because we are forgiven. The Bible asks "if God is for you, then who can be against you?" (Rom. 8:31). The answer is, no one, including yourself. If God has forgiven you, then why can't or why won't you forgive yourself?

Forgiving yourself releases you to be who you were created to be, and forgiving others that have hurt you is more about your personal healing than it is their healing. We were not made to be bitter but free. I encourage you to complete an inventory of those who have hurt you and those whom you have hurt. Then turn all of it over to God. Stop holding onto it as an excuse to stay broken, and let God take your mess and make a masterpiece.

DAY 64
WORTHY

> *Ephesians 4:1-3*
>
> *"¹ As a prisoner for the Lord, then, I urge you to live a life worthy of the calling you have received. ² Be completely humble and gentle; be patient, bearing with one another in love. ³ Make every effort to keep the unity of the Spirit through the bond of peace."*

We read in our passage today that we are to live a life worthy of our calling, and then we read some characteristics that should be prevalent in that kind of life. It continues to explain that we are to be humble, gentle, patient, treat each other with love and that all we do should be done in love. Finally, we are told to keep our Christian family's unity and peace. This passage shares how we should live and it serves as a call to action for all believers. Our lives are not to be passive, moved by what society finds acceptable, but active, stable, and a beacon in the darkness of our world. Each one of us that are believers has a higher purpose. We are called to live like Christ, to love like Christ, and to keep unity and peace like Christ. This calling is a mantel placed upon us when we accept Jesus as our Lord and Savior, the moment we are born again. As we dive deeper into this passage, we will see the characteristics of this calling are humility, gentleness, patience, love, and unity.

At the beginning of this verse, Paul identifies himself as a prisoner of the Lord. Understand he was not in jail for committing an awful crime of some sort. He was only in jail because of his unwavering commitment to the Gospel of Christ. He was willing to suffer for the sake of the Gospel, and he implores us to do the same. In other words, he is saying that we must be willing to surrender comfort, acceptance, and even relationships for the sake of Christ. In fact, if we aren't willing to suffer for the sake of God's Glory, then we are probably nowhere close to where we need to be in our relationship with God. This does not necessarily mean physical suffering, but rather, it means we must be willing to sacrifice our own desires for the sake of Christ and His Kingdom.

The first characteristic of the calling listed is humility. Paul says we must walk with all lowliness. Humility is the opposite of pride and is essential in order for us to be effective in our Christian walk. When we are humble, we recognize we are not the center of the universe and that our needs and desires are not the most important thing. Instead, we are to put others first and seek to serve them. The second characteristic listed is gentleness. We are to walk with all gentleness, which means we are to be kind, compassionate, and understanding towards others. This is especially important when dealing with those who are weaker or vulnerable. Gentleness is not weakness, but rather, it is strength under control. When we are gentle, we demonstrate the love of Christ towards others, and we create an environment where people feel safe and cared for. The third characteristic is patience. We are to be patient with others, even when they are challenging to deal with. Patience is the ability to endure hardship without losing our faith or our temper. It is a fruit of the Spirit that is essential for us to bear, especially when dealing with those who are different from us or have different opinions. The fourth characteristic is love. We are to bear with one another in love. Love is the foundation of all Christian virtues and is the most essential characteristic of the Christian life. Love is not just a feeling but a choice we make every day to put others first and seek their well-being. When we love others, we imitate Christ, who loved us so much that He gave His life for us. The final characteristic is unity. We are to endeavor to keep the unity of the Spirit through the bond of peace. Unity does not mean uniformity; instead, it means we are to be united in our faith and commitment to Christ. We are all part of the same body and have a role to play. When we are united, we are stronger and more effective in fulfilling the mission Christ has given us.

Changed

Day 64 Exercises

1. What is your calling?

2. What changes must be made in your life to live a life worthy of your calling?

3. What would be different about your life if you applied all aspects of this verse to it?

4. Explain unity and how you can be instrumental in unifying other believers.

DAY 65
OVERCOMER

> *1 John 5:4*
>
> *"for everyone born of God overcomes the world. This is the victory that has overcome the world, even our faith."*

Today's verse speaks to the power of faith in our lives and how it enables us to overcome the obstacles and challenges we face in the world. When we become born again and enter into a relationship with God, we are given the power to overcome the world. This means our struggles and trials do not have to defeat us. We do not have to stay stuck in sins that have defeated us, nor do we have to succumb to temptation. Through Christ, we have the strength, ability, and courage we need to face them head-on because we know God is with us every step of the way.

We must live our lives by faith because it is the key that unlocks the door to God's power in our lives. When we believe in God's promises and trust in His goodness, we are able to overcome anything that comes our way.

Our world is full of challenges and temptations that can easily overwhelm us. We are bombarded with messages telling us to pursue material possessions, seek pleasure at all costs, and put our desires above all else. As believers, we know these things are empty and ultimately unsatisfying. We know true fulfillment can only be found in our relationship with God.

Faith enables us to see beyond the fleeting pleasures of this world and focus on God's eternal promises. It gives us the courage to say no to temptation and to resist the lies of the enemy. It empowers us to walk in obedience to God's commands and to live a life that is pleasing to Him. We are not stuck doing the same old things over and over again. We are promised to be overcomers.

We need to understand that faith is not just a one-time decision we make. It is an ongoing journey of trust and dependence on God. It requires us to constantly turn our hearts towards Him and seek His will in all we do. When we do this, we can experience the fullness of His power in our lives, which produces the victory we need.

The only way we will have strong enough faith to overcome the world is by spending time in God's Word, in prayer, and in fellowship with other believers. These practices help us stay connected to God and accountable to one another, enabling us to encourage each other through life's journey. By ourselves, we can do nothing; we need God's help, and we need each other in order to reach the place He desires us to be.

Faith in God allows us to face the challenges of life with confidence and hope. We know no matter what happens, God is with us and has a plan for our lives. We can trust in His goodness and faithfulness, even when we don't understand what is happening around us. He indeed does have our best interests at heart.

Changed

Day 65 Exercises

1. Share the worldly behaviors and habits you need to overcome.

___

2. What steps do you think you can take to be victorious over the behaviors and habits listed above?

___

3. How do you feel about only God being able to help you overcome?

___

4. What steps must you take to allow God to make you an overcomer?

___

DAY 66
STRIVE

> *2 Peter 1:10*
>
> *"Therefore, my brothers and sisters, make every effort to confirm your calling and election. For if you do these things, you will never stumble."*

This verse is an important reminder for all believers. It reminds us our faith is not static or passive. Instead, it requires effort and intentionality on our part. We must confirm our calling and election. This confirmation is found in how we live our lives and the degree of our faith.

The first part of this verse says to "make every effort." This implies we should be diligent and intentional in pursuing God. We should not be content to simply rest on our past experiences or assume our faith will just naturally grow on its own. Instead, we must take ownership of our faith and actively seek to deepen our relationship with God. One way we can do this is by regularly spending time in prayer and reading God's Word. We can't expect to grow in our faith if we're not regularly engaging with the source of our faith. So, we must make time for God in our daily lives and intentionally seek Him.

Another way we can make every effort to confirm our calling and election is by being intentional about our relationships with other believers. We are not meant to live out our faith in isolation. We need the support and encouragement of other believers to help us grow and stay on track. We need to seek out opportunities for fellowship, discipleship, and accountability with other believers. The first part of this speaks about the calling and election we are told to make every effort to confirm. It says that if we do these things, we will never stumble. This doesn't mean we will never face difficulties or challenges, but that we will be able to remain steadfast in our faith and not be shaken when we do.

When we confirm our calling and election, we are essentially anchoring ourselves in God's truth and promises. We are building our faith on a solid foundation that cannot be shaken. This gives us the strength and resilience to withstand whatever challenges come our way. One of the key ways we can confirm our calling and election is by being obedient to God's Word. We demonstrate our faith and trust in Him when we obey God's commands. We are also building our faith on a solid foundation that cannot be shaken. Obedience to God's Word is not always easy. It often requires us to step outside of our comfort zones and do difficult or uncomfortable things. Nevertheless, our obedience to God confirms our faith, calling, and election. It is how we show we believe His ways are better than ours and that His plans for us are good.

Another way we can confirm our calling and election is by persevering through trials and hardships. When we face difficult circumstances, it can be tempting to give up on our faith or to doubt God's goodness. But our perseverance shows our faith and trust in God are true. Perseverance builds our faith and strengthens our relationship with God. It reminds us we are not alone in our struggles and that God is always with us, even amid our pain and suffering. Finally, we can confirm our calling and election by sharing our faith with others. When we share the Gospel with others, we show that we trust in God and help others find hope and salvation in Jesus Christ.

Changed

Day 66 Exercises

1. What are you called to do for the Lord?

2. What can you do to make every effort to confirm your calling and election?

3. Why do you or why do you not feel that your election and calling has been confirmed?

4. How does it make you feel to understand the hardships of this life give us opportunities to confirm our faith?

DAY 67

HANG ON

> *2 John 1:8*
>
> *"Watch out that you do not lose what we have worked for, but that you may be rewarded fully."*

Today's short verse is a powerful reminder to pay attention to our walk with God so we don't lose what we have worked for. It is so easy in life to get carried away by its concerns as well as our own personal wants and desires. Even so, we are instructed in today's verse that if we continue in obedience to God, we will receive the full reward He has planned. Nothing good generally happens by accident. We have to be intentional. Today's verse reminds believers of the importance of staying vigilant and faithful in our walk with God.

Throughout the book of Second John, we see John express his love and concern for those he is writing to. He consistently urges them to continue in the truth they have heard from the beginning, not to lose heart, and to obey the Lord consistently.

The verse begins with a warning to watch ourselves; it is really up to each of us to pay attention to where we are physically, spiritually, and emotionally. If we aren't careful, we can be sidetracked by good intentions, basic needs, or even worse. The phrase "watch out" is a command to be on guard against spiritual danger. Just as a guard watches over his assignment to protect it from danger, we, too, must guard our spiritual lives against the attack of the flesh and the enemy.

The fact that we are told to be careful of losing what we have worked for does not necessarily refer to one's salvation but to the abundant life we are promised. If we aren't careful to live in obedience, we will lose our progress in our relationship with God. This loss will result in a hindrance to the fruit of the Spirit being manifest in our lives. Suffering from lack of love, joy, peace, and so forth will hinder the "full reward" God has prepared for us.

We must be careful not to be deceived by false teachings, led away by natural desires, or fall into sin. These are real dangers all believers face. "Watching out" is being vigilant, active, and intentional not to fall away. The phrase "rewarded fully" is a promise of the blessings and benefits that come from a faithful and obedient life with God, the manifestation of the fruit of His Spirit in our lives.

Staying grounded in the truth of God's Word and connected to the body of Christ, through fellowshipping with other believers who can encourage and keep us accountable is vital to "watching out."

Guarding our hearts against sin and cultivating a heart of obedience is also essential to maintaining a walk with God that will produce the "full reward." Being obedient to God is not always easy, but it is always worth it. We can be confident we will not lose what we have worked for but that we will receive the full reward of a life lived in fellowship with Him if we remain in Him.

Changed

Day 67 Exercises

1. What full rewards are promised to you by God through His Word?

2. Do your desires line up with God's full rewards? Explain why or why not.

3. Explain what "watching out" means to you.

4. Explain the tragedy of not having the abundant life promised to you because you were not careful to live in obedience.

DAY 68

HE DID IT

> *2 Timothy 1:9*
>
> *"He has saved us and called us to a holy life not because of anything we have done but because of his own purpose and grace. This grace was given us in Christ Jesus before the beginning of time."*

Our verse today states: "He has saved us and called us to a holy life not because of anything we have done but because of His own purpose and grace." We do not earn this grace, but it is given to us as a free gift when we accept Christ as our Savior. God's grace is great, amazing, and free to us. Having God's grace is not based on anything we have done or because we have earned it in any way. Instead, God simply loves us because we are His creation, and because of such, He has given us grace in Christ Jesus since before the beginning of time."

Paul reminds us in today's verse that God's grace is not just a one-time gift of salvation that cleanses us from our sins but a continuous flow of undeserved favor. This grace favors and sustains us throughout life's journey. His grace empowers us to live a holy life, not because of our efforts but because of God's purpose.

We must first understand salvation is not something we can earn. We cannot work hard enough or be good enough to deserve it. It is a gift God freely gives us, motivated solely by His love for us. This grace is not just for the "good" people or those who have it all together. It is for all of us, no matter how broken or lost we may feel.

When we accept His gift of salvation, we also accept God's call on our lives. He has a purpose for each one of us, and that purpose is to live a holy life. This does not mean that we are expected to be perfect, but rather that we are striving to be more like Christ every day. We are called to love God and others, serve and give, and share the Good News of Jesus with those around us.

The amazing thing about God's grace is that it is not just for the present moment. It was given to us before the beginning of time; meaning it extends into our past and future. God's grace is available to us even before we know we need it, and it will continue to sustain us long after we have left this physical life. It changes everything when we truly grasp the depth of God's grace. We no longer have to live in fear or anxiety about our salvation or our ability to live a holy life. Instead, we can trust that God has already given us everything we need in order to walk in His ways.

This does not mean we will never struggle or face challenges, but it means we have a source of strength and hope that is greater than anything in this world. Remember, we are saved not because of our efforts but because of His great love for us. Embrace His call to live a holy life, knowing His grace will sustain you every step of the way. Rest in the assurance that His grace covers you entirely: past, present, and future.

Changed

Day 68 Exercises

1. In what ways has your life not been holy?

_____
_____
_____
_____
_____
_____
_____

2. How does God's grace given to you allow you to leave behind those behaviors listed above?

_____
_____
_____
_____
_____
_____
_____

3. Describe what your life looks like with God's grace empowering Holiness in you?

_____
_____
_____
_____
_____
_____
_____

4. What does it mean to you that His Holiness in you is not based on anything you can do?

_____
_____
_____
_____
_____
_____
_____

DAY 69

PURE

> *1 Thessalonians 4:7*
>
> *"For God did not call us to be impure, but to live a holy life."*

Today's verse states: "For God did not call us to be impure, but to live a holy life." Simply put, God expects His children to live a holy life. As we learned yesterday, this Holiness is based on what He has done. Holiness means to be set apart, pure, and righteous. As Christians, we are called to live a life that reflects the character of God. We are not to live the same way the world does. We are to be peculiar and different, to stand out. The only way we can live a life is pleasing to God is to allow Him to live through us and to be like Him. It is not enough to simply believe in God and go about our lives as we please. We must live a life that strives to display His Holiness and reflects His love and grace.

Living a life of Holiness requires us to make some difficult choices:

1. We must follow God's commands even when they are difficult or unpopular.
2. We must flee sin and temptation and pursue righteousness and purity instead.
3. We must put aside our desires and seek to glorify God in all we do.

Being set apart is not always an easy path to follow. The world around us is filled with temptation and sin. It can be easy to fall into the trap of living for our own pleasure and desires. But when we choose to live a life of Holiness, we are choosing to follow God's plan for our lives. We are choosing to trust in His wisdom and guidance, even when we don't understand why things are happening the way they are.

It also means we must be intentional in our relationships. We must choose to surround ourselves with people who will encourage us in our walk with God. We must choose to build relationships that will challenge us to grow in our faith and become more like Christ. We must also be willing to let go of relationships that are leading us away from God. As we strive to live a life of Holiness, we can take comfort in the fact that God is with us every step of the way. He has given us the Holy Spirit to guide and empower us. We can also take comfort in the knowledge of we are not alone in our pursuit of Holiness. We are part of a community of believers who are all striving to live a life that pleases God.

Living a holy life is not a suggestion or a recommendation but a command from God. As we seek to follow God's plan, we must remember that living a life of Holiness is not just about our personal growth and development. It is also about being a witness to the world around us. When we live a life of Holiness, we are showing others what it means to follow Christ. We are showing them the love and grace of God. While it is not always easy to live the oly life that God has planned for us, it is always worth it; no matter how difficult the choices may be or the sacrifices will be required. Our obedience will produce a life that is more Christ-like. It will bring us closer to God and allow us to experience His love and grace.

Changed

Day 69 Exercises

1. How do you feel about God's expectation for you to live a holy life?

2. Are there things that hinder Holiness in your life? (Relationships, habits, desires, etc..)

3. How will you achieve God's exceptions of you?

4. Why is it important to live a life that reflects God's love, grace and Holiness?

DAY 70

HOLY

> *1 Peter 1:15-16*
>
> *"15 But just as he who called you is holy, so be holy in all you do; 16 for it is written: "Be holy, because I am holy.""*

Our topic today seems to be keeping with the theme of holiness. 1 Peter 1:15-16 says, "But just as He who called you is holy, so be holy in all you do; for it is written: 'Be holy because I am holy.'" This passage is another call to live a holy life in all aspects, just as God is holy.

We have already addressed the fact that holiness is not simply being morally upright or doing good deeds. Instead, holiness is the state of being set apart for God's purposes and living in accordance with His will. It involves obedience and requires us to live a life that pleases God. We are called to live a life that reflects His character, a life that will be a testimony for Him and draw those who are far from God back to Him. A holy life is essential to fulfilling the Great Commission.

In this passage, Peter reminds us that God is the One who has called us to live a holy life. Holiness is not something we achieve on our own through our own efforts or good works. Instead, as we have discussed already, it is something that God has called us to do, and it is through His power and grace that we are able to live it out.

The call to be holy in all we do means we are to live a life set apart from the world and its values in every area of our life. We are not to compartmentalize our lives and just give God portions of ourselves, but we are to surrender our whole beings, wants, desires, and actions. We are commanded to live in a way that is pleasing to God. This will require us to go against the norms and values of society. Standing up for what is right and living a life that is characterized by selflessness and sacrifice will cost us everything.

We must intentionally pursue a deeper relationship with God and allow Him to work in our lives so that He will mold us into His image. Living a holy life is not something that can be achieved overnight. It requires commitment, ongoing growth, and being transformed into His likeness. Living a good life, being a good person, and even being respected in our community does not equate to Holiness. God's standards are far higher than mankind's. As the Scriptures state, His ways are not our ways, and His thoughts are not our thoughts (Isaiah 55:8-9). We are to meet the standard that belongs to God.

The Good News is that we are not alone in this journey; God has given us His Spirit to empower and guide us along the way. As we submit to His leading and allow Him to work in our lives, we will begin to see the fruit of the Spirit growing in us – love, joy, peace, patience, kindness, goodness, faithfulness, gentleness, and self-control (Galatians 5:22-23). This will set us apart from this world and make us holy as He is holy.

Changed

Day 70 Exercises

1. Describe God's standard for holiness.

2. Explain the effect of having the Holy Spirit within you to help you reach God's expectations.

3. List the reasons why you may not be able to be holy as He is holy.

4. How does the fruit of the Spirit set you apart from the world?

Week 11

> *"Ask yourself if who you are is defined by what you do or if what you do is defined by who you are."*

We have a Creator, and He has given us an identity. Unfortunately, many of us have not been fulfilling our purpose because we haven't been right with God. When we are transformed and begin to live as believers in Christ, we step out of the deception we have been living in and into who we were truly designed to be.

Living in our new, profound transformation through our faith in Jesus delivers us from the eternal consequences of our past mistakes and insecurities. This identity is not indecisive, as it is firmly rooted in Him and shapes our character and behavior. Let's look at a few universal identities and their implications for all believers.

A Child of God: The moment we accept Jesus as our Lord and Savior, we become children of God. We are adopted into His family, and our identity is forever changed. Our character should reflect this truth by displaying the love, grace, and kindness that God lavishes upon us. We are called to treat others with compassion and seek reconciliation, just as our Heavenly Father did for us.

Chosen and Called: In Christ, we are chosen and called for a specific purpose. We are not accidents or mere spectators in life; God has uniquely designed us to bring glory to His name. Our lives should reflect this calling by behaving intentionally and making choices that align with God's will. We are called to pursue righteousness, serve others selflessly, and use our gifts and talents to honor Him.

Forgiven and Redeemed: Through the sacrifice of Jesus on the cross, we are forgiven and redeemed. Our past mistakes and sins no longer define us. God's grace covers our shortcomings and His mercy provides a fresh start. As recipients of such great love, our character should exhibit humility and gratitude. We should extend forgiveness to others and embrace the freedom and joy that come from being made new in Christ.

Victorious in Christ: In Christ, we are more than conquerors. The battles we face may be challenging, but our victory is assured because of the One who lives within us. Our behavior should reflect this truth by displaying faith, perseverance, and unwavering trust in God's promises. We are called to stand firm in the face of adversity, knowing the victory has already been won through Christ's finished work on the cross.

Changed

Ambassadors of Christ: As believers, we are ambassadors of Christ, entrusted with the responsibility to represent Him in this world. Our character should reflect the character of our Heavenly King. We should strive for integrity, honesty, and righteousness in all areas of our lives. Our behavior should be marked by love, compassion, and a genuine concern for the well-being of others. Through our words and actions we have the privilege of leading others to encounter the transforming power of Christ.

Our identity in Christ defines who we are, what we do, and how we live. Our character and behavior should reflect the truth that we are children of God; chosen and called, forgiven and redeemed, victorious in Christ, and ambassadors of His love. Let us embrace our identity in Him, allowing it to shape every aspect of our lives. May we continually seek His guidance and rely on His strength to walk in a manner worthy of our calling. As we do so, we will experience the fullness of a life that comes from living in alignment with our true identity in Christ.

DAY 71
FIRST PLACE

> *Deuteronomy 6:5*
>
> *"Love the Lord your God with all your heart and with all your soul and with all your strength."*

This verse is one of the most well-known and significant verses in the entire Old Testament. The command within this verse is derived from the first three commands of the Ten Commandments.

1. "You shall have no other gods before me."

2. "You shall make no idols."

3. "You shall not take the name of the Lord your God in vain."

As you can see, our verse today states, "You shall love the Lord your God with all your heart, with all your soul, and with all your strength." This cannot be achieved without honoring His first three commands.

What this verse is calling us to have is total devotion to God. It is a reminder that our relationship with God is not meant to be casual or half-hearted. Rather, we are called to love God with every fiber of our being. This means our love for God should be all-encompassing and should guide every aspect of our lives.

To truly love God with all our heart, soul, and strength requires a deep understanding of who God is and what He has done for us. It means recognizing that God is the Creator of the universe, the Source of all goodness and love, and the One who has saved us from sin. It means acknowledging that we owe everything to God and living our lives in gratitude of His mercy and grace.

Loving God with all our hearts also requires us to prioritize our relationship with Him above all else. This means setting aside time each day to pray, read the Bible, and seek His guidance. It means making choices honor God and seeking to please Him in all we do. It means putting God first in our thoughts, words, and actions, even when it may be difficult or unpopular.

To love God with all our souls means to love Him with the very essence of who we are. It means loving Him not just with our physical bodies but with our emotions, desires, and will. It means allowing God to transform us from the inside out so we become more and more like Him every day. It means surrendering our desires and plans to God's will and trusting Him to lead us in the best way.

Finally, to love God with all our strength means using our physical and mental abilities to serve Him and bring glory to His name. It means using our talents and resources to bless others and advance His Kingdom. It means working hard and doing our best in all we do, knowing that we are ultimately working for God and not for ourselves.

Changed

Day 71 Exercises

1. How has your life not shown that you love God above all else?

2. How has your life shown that you do love God above all else?

3. What do you feel God expects in order for your life to look like a life spent with Him?

4. Describe how you will commit your life to loving God above all else.

DAY 72
LOVING OTHERS

> *Matthew 22:37-40*
>
> *"37 And he said to him, "You shall love the Lord your God with all your heart and with all your soul and with all your mind. 38 This is the great and first commandment. 39 And a second is like it: You shall love your neighbor as yourself. 40 On these two commandments depend all the Law and the Prophets."*

Our passage today records one of the most famous exchanges between Jesus and one of the religious leaders of His day. When asked by this leader what the greatest commandment is, Jesus shared: "Love the Lord your God with all your heart, with all your soul, and with all your mind." Yet, He didn't end it there.

Jesus went on to share that the second greatest commandment is to love our neighbor as ourselves. This means we are to treat others with the same love, respect, and kindness we want. We are to try and meet their needs, to care for them, to help them when they are hurting, and to share our hope in Christ Jesus with them.

Love is not optional! Love is not just a nice sentiment, a pitter-patter of the heart, or even a physical desire. Love is at the very heart of what it means to follow Jesus. In fact, Jesus said that all the Law and the Prophets, the entire Old Testament, are summed up in these two commandments. If we get these two things right - loving God and loving others - everything else will fall into place.

The ability to love others the way God desires is something that flows out of our love for God. When we love God with all our heart, soul, and mind, we will naturally love our neighbor as ourselves. This love won't have to be mustered up or manufactured it will be a natural by-product of our love for God.

To love our neighbor as ourselves means treating others with the same love, respect, and kindness that we would want for ourselves. It means that we seek to meet their needs, care for them when they are hurting, and share our hope in Christ with them. This kind of love extends not just to our friends and family but to everyone we come into contact with - even our enemies. God's love truly has no boundaries.

Promise Land's vision is to reach the lost for Christ, meet the needs of our community, and impact our world with His love, truth, and grace. This is love in action. We would do well to know love is an action word. Claiming to love others but not having action is of little value. We are reminded of this in the book of James, when He declares, that he will show his faith by what he does. Everything we do should be bound by God's love for mankind.

I find it a lot easier to love those who are difficult when I take the time to remember God loves them and He paid the penalty for their sins. I will venture to say if you don't love others, then you don't love God. After all, the Bible says in John 13:35 "By this, all men will know that you are My disciples if you have love for one another.

Changed

Day 72 Exercises

1. In what ways does your life show you love God?

2. In what ways does your life show you are not loving God like you should?

3. List ways you, personally, can "reach the lost for Christ and impact your world with love, truth, and grace.".

4. How could you show God you love Him above everyone and everything else?

DAY 73

DEBT-FREE

> *Romans 13:8*
>
> *"Let no debt remain outstanding, except the continuing debt to love one another, for whoever loves others has fulfilled the law."*

Today's verse states: "Let no debt remain outstanding, except the continuing debt to love one another, for whoever loves others has fulfilled the law." This verse speaks to the idea of fulfilling our responsibilities to one another. Our God expects us to treat others with love as He has treated us. We owe others the same love God has shown us.

In the preceding verses, Paul speaks about the role of government and the importance of submitting to authorities. We would do well to remember there are no authorities or powers except by God's design. In today's verse, Paul shifts the focus from our role with leadership to our personal relationships. He reminds us that we have a debt of love to one another. This debt is one that we can never fully repay. Love is not just a feeling. It is an action. We are called to love actively and sacrificially, giving of ourselves for the benefit of others.

When we love others, we fulfill God's law. Jesus taught that all of the law and the prophets could be summed up in two commands: to love God and our neighbor as ourselves (Matthew 22:37-40). Love is the foundation of our relationship with God and with others. Love serves as the mark of a true disciple of Christ. Paul defines love in 1 Corinthians 13: Love is patient and kind. It does not envy or boast. It is not arrogant or rude. Love does not insist on its own way. It is not irritable or resentful. Love bears all things, believes all things, hopes all things, and endures all things. Love never ends.

This is the kind of love we are called to show others. We are called to be selfless and sacrificial. We are to put others' needs before our own. We are to build up and encourage others. This is love in action. We are to love the unlovable. Our love is based on God; it is not to be dependent on whether the other person deserves it or not or if we feel like it. Our love is to be a love that reflects the character of God. When we love others in this way, we demonstrate the reality of the Gospel. Jesus Himself said that the world would know we are his disciples by our love (John 13:35). Our love for one another is a powerful statement of faith and witness to the world. It is a reflection of the love God has for us.

It is not always easy to love. There are people in our lives who are difficult to love. They may have different beliefs or values than we do, or may have even hurt us in the past. It can be tempting to hold grudges or to avoid these people altogether. But this is not the kind of love we are called to show. Jesus calls us to love our enemies and to pray for those who persecute us (Matthew 5:44). This is a radical kind of love that goes against our natural inclinations. It is a love that requires us to lay down our pride and forgive those who have wronged us. It is a love that is only possible through the power of the Holy Spirit.

Remember, the passage today says love is our debt to one another. This means we owe it to them. Giving someone what they are owed is not treating them special. It is giving them what they deserve. We should always try to remember treating others with love, and caring for them as God does, is an expected bare minimum, not the extravagant.

Changed

Day 73 Exercises

1. Explain the phrase "debt of love."

   _____
   _____
   _____
   _____
   _____
   _____
   _____
   _____

2. How has God shown His love towards others and you?

   _____
   _____
   _____
   _____
   _____
   _____
   _____
   _____

3. In what ways does your love reflect God's love?

   _____
   _____
   _____
   _____
   _____
   _____
   _____
   _____

4. What can you do to better show God's love to others?

   _____
   _____
   _____
   _____
   _____
   _____
   _____
   _____

DAY 74
HUMILITY

> *Philippians 2:3*
>
> *"Do nothing out of selfish ambition or vain conceit. Rather, in humility value others above yourselves."*

In this letter to the Philippians, the apostle Paul captures the essence of selfless love. Philippians 2:3 reminds believers to shift their focus from self-centeredness to a Christ-like attitude of humility and genuine concern for others. In a world that often encourages self-promotion and personal gain, this verse presents a radical perspective on how we are called to live as followers of Christ.

Paul begins by encouraging us to reject two harmful traits: selfish ambition and vain conceit. Selfish ambition arises from a mindset that is solely focused on personal gain and advancement. It drives individuals to pursue their own interests, often disregarding the needs and well-being of those around them. Vain conceit, on the other hand, stems from an inflated sense of self-importance, where one's own desires and opinions take precedence over others.

As followers of Christ, we are called to a higher standard. Instead of being motivated by self-centered ambitions and pride, we are to live humbly, considering others more significant than ourselves. This humility is not a false modesty or a devaluation of our own worth but a genuine recognition that every person, regardless of their status or background, is deserving of love, respect, and care. The path to selfless love begins with transforming our hearts and minds. It requires us to surrender our own agendas and desires at the feet of Jesus, allowing His love to permeate every aspect of our lives. When we align our hearts with Christ, we begin to see others through His eyes and value them as He does.

One of the most significant challenges we face in practicing selfless love is overcoming our backgrounds and the cultural norms we have grown accustomed to. Our society often celebrates individual achievements and material success, leaving little room for genuine concern for others. However, as believers, we are called to be counter-cultural, peculiar, strange, and a shining beacon of Christ's love in a world that desperately needs it. Selfless love is not a one-time act but a lifelong commitment. It manifests itself in the way we treat others daily, in both big and small ways. It means setting aside our own preferences and comforts to uplift and serve those around us. It means listening attentively to others, showing empathy, and extending a helping hand when needed. It means sacrificing our time, resources, and even our own interests to meet the needs of others.

The example of Christ Himself is the ultimate inspiration for selfless love. Jesus, the Son of God, willingly humbled Himself, leaving the glories of Heaven to dwell among us. He washed His disciples' feet, healed the sick, and showed compassion to the less thans. Ultimately, Jesus demonstrated the greatest act of selfless love by laying down His life on the cross, bearing the weight of our sins so we could experience redemption and eternal life. As we reflect on Philippians 2:3, let us reevaluate our attitudes and actions. Let us strive to cultivate a heart of humility and selflessness, imitating the very nature of Christ. May we reject the allure of selfish ambition and vain conceit and instead value others above ourselves. By doing so, we can be instruments of God's transformative love in the lives of those around us, bringing hope, healing, and reconciliation to a broken world.

Changed

Day 74 Exercises

1. What selfish ambitions and vain conceits are in your life?

2. How will you surrender the above to Jesus?

3. What differences will be in your life when you begin to value others over self?

4. How does a humble lifestyle portray Christ?

DAY 75
FIRST & SECOND

> *Matthew 5:43-45*
>
> *"⁴³ You have heard that it was said, 'Love your neighbor[a] and hate your enemy.' ⁴⁴ But I tell you, love your enemies and pray for those who persecute you, ⁴⁵ that you may be children of your Father in Heaven."*

Our passage today is an important reminder of the transformative power of love. It challenges us to love not only our friends and neighbors but also our enemies and those who seek to harm us. Unfortunately, loving like this is not the norm. We are often taught to avoid or get back at those who have wronged us. Jesus taught us by and through His own example. As followers Jesus, we are to love the unlovable. This is not an easy task. It goes against our natural human instincts and requires us to transcend our desires and emotions.

The passage begins with Jesus quoting the popular wisdom of the time, "Love your neighbor and hate your enemy." This was a common way of thinking in the culture of that day and age and still is even today. It is natural to want to protect oneself and to prioritize the needs of one's own community. Yet Jesus dismantles this way of thinking. Instead, He instructs His followers to love their enemies and pray for those who persecute them. This command is not just a suggestion. Jesus tells us that in order to be "children of our Father," we must love our enemies. As disciples of Christ, our goal should remain to be His children. When we love others, even those who would seek to harm us, we demonstrate the love and grace of God in a powerful way. We become a reflection of His character and His love for all people.

But how do we love our enemies? This is a difficult question and one that has challenged believers ever since Jesus taught us to love as He does. It requires us to go beyond our emotions and desires and see each individual as God sees them. We must understand that Jesus died for them, loves them, and longs to guide them into His Kingdom. We must show compassion and kindness, even in the face of adversity. After all, if those who hate us find Jesus, then they, too, will love with His love. One way to love our enemies is through prayer. Jesus tells us to pray for those who persecute us. Praying for those who have hurt us requires us to let go of our anger and bitterness. We should instead seek the good of those who would harm us. Praying for our enemies may or may not change them, but it will always change us. Our hearts will become open instead of closed off, and we will be filled with God's love; a powerful love that transforms us from the inside out. Our hearts will be softened, our anger subdued, and we will be moved with compassion and kindness.

Another way to love our enemies is through acts of kindness and service. Jesus tells us to go the extra mile, to turn the other cheek, and to give to those who would take from us. It requires us to let go of our desires and prioritize the needs of others. We demonstrate God's love by showing kindness and compassion to all, even our enemies. We become a light in the darkness, showing others there is a better way to live. Ultimately, loving our enemies is a way of breaking the cycle of hate and violence. When we respond to hate with love, we demonstrate there is another way to live. We show it is possible to overcome our own emotions and desires and live in a spirit of compassion and kindness. We become agents of transformation, helping to bring about a more just and peaceful world. As we seek to love our enemies, we can draw inspiration from the example of Christ Himself. He showed us the ultimate example of love, giving His life on the cross for the sake of all people, even those who would seek to harm Him. May we all strive to love our enemies and pray for those persecuting us. May we seek to be agents of transformation in the world, reflecting the love and grace of our Father in Heaven in all that we are.

Changed

Day 75 Exercises

1. Who has been your enemy and why?

_____

2. What is God telling you about your relationship with those listed above?

_____

3. Ask God to reveal people and situations that you need to forgive and list them here.

_____

4. Explain how you will safely extend and seek forgiveness from those whom you may have harmed.

_____

DAY 76
CALLED

> *Matthew 28:19-20*
>
> *"*^{19}* Therefore go and make disciples of all nations, baptizing them in the name of the Father and of the Son and of the Holy Spirit, *^{20}* and teaching them to obey everything I have commanded you. And surely I am with you always, to the very end of the age."*

Our passage today comes from the closing words of Jesus in the Gospel of Matthew. This is known as the Great Commission. Jesus' words serve as a powerful mandate given to the disciples and to us. These verses serve as a rallying cry for all believers across time and space, as they outline our primary mission as followers of Christ: to make disciples. Let us consider the call to "go." Jesus' command challenges us to move beyond our comfort zones and engage with the world around us. It compels us to step out in faith and actively seek opportunities to share the love and truth of the Gospel. Our faith should not be confined within the walls of our churches. Instead, we are called to be the hands and feet of Jesus in a broken world.

As we go, we are to make disciples of all nations. Discipleship involves more than simply sharing the Good News of salvation; it requires investing our time, energy, and resources into nurturing and guiding others in their journey of faith. It is a process of leading others to a personal relationship with Christ and helping them grow in their understanding of Him. We are called to walk alongside fellow believers, encouraging and challenging them to become more like Jesus in every aspect of their lives. The act of baptizing symbolizes the public declaration of one's faith in Jesus Christ. Baptism marks the beginning of a new life in Christ, where old sins are washed away, and we are raised to walk in the newness of life. It is a visible sign of our identification with Christ and our commitment to follow Him wholeheartedly. Through baptism, we participate in God's redemptive work, sharing in the joy of seeing lives transformed by His grace.

Moreover, discipleship involves teaching others to obey everything that Jesus commanded. It requires imparting the truths of God's Word and helping believers grow in their knowledge and understanding of the Scriptures. We are entrusted with the responsibility of equipping others to live according to the teachings of Christ, empowering them to make choices that align with His will. Teaching is essential to discipleship, for it equips and enables believers to mature in their faith and become effective witnesses for Christ. The closing promise of Jesus in this passage brings great assurance to every disciple: "And surely, I am with you always, to the very end of the age" (Matt. 28:20). As we embark on the mission of making disciples, we are not alone. The omnipotent presence of Jesus accompanies us every step of the way. He is our constant source of strength, guidance, and comfort. In the face of challenges, doubts, and uncertainties, we can draw confidence from the fact that Jesus is with us, empowering us by the Holy Spirit to fulfill the Great Commission.

Today, let us reflect on the Great Commission and examine our own commitment to discipleship. Are we actively engaged in making disciples, or have we grown complacent? Are we intentional about investing in the lives of others, helping them grow in their faith? Are we obediently teaching and modeling the ways of Christ to those around us? May we be renewed in our passion to fulfill the Great Commission. Let us be bold and courageous, stepping out in faith to share the love of Christ with those around us. May we prioritize discipleship, walking alongside fellow believers and helping them grow in their relationship with Jesus. And let us take comfort in the promise that Jesus is with us, empowering us as we fulfill our calling until the very end of the age.

Changed

Day 76 Exercises

1. Explain the Great Commission In your own words.

_____
_____
_____
_____
_____
_____
_____

2. Why is it important for all believers to be a part of this commission?

_____
_____
_____
_____
_____
_____
_____
_____

3. How can you participate in fulfilling this call in your life?

_____
_____
_____
_____
_____
_____
_____
_____

4. What limitations in your life may hinder your fulfillment of this passage and how will you overcome them?

_____
_____
_____
_____
_____
_____
_____
_____

DAY 77

RULE

> *Psalm 8:6*
> *"You made them rulers over the works of Your hands; You put everything under their feet."*

Psalm 8 is a majestic hymn that exalts the glory and splendor of God's creation. In our verse today, the psalmist marvels at the divine act of granting mankind authority and dominion over the works of God's hands. This verse highlights the privilege bestowed upon humanity and reminds us of the responsibility that comes with this position of stewardship. When we gaze upon the vastness of the universe, with its countless galaxies and celestial bodies, we cannot help but feel small and insignificant. Yet, in His infinite wisdom, God has chosen to entrust us with a unique role in His creation. We are not mere spectators; we have been appointed rulers over His hands' works.

This authority, however, is not intended for our selfish ambitions or to assert dominion over others. Rather, it is a call to stewardship—a responsibility to care for and cultivate the world God has entrusted to us. We are called to be caretakers of His creation, exercising our dominion with wisdom, humility, and reverence. As rulers over the works of God's hands, we can impact the world in profound ways. Our influence extends beyond the natural realm and encompasses the spheres of our relationships, communities, and endeavors. We are called to bring God's Kingdom values to bear in every area of our lives, reflecting His character and goodness to those around us.

To understand the significance of this responsibility, we must recognize the inherent value and beauty of all creation. Every aspect of the world around us—the mountains and oceans, the animals and plants—testifies to our Heavenly Father's creative power and love. Each living being bears the imprint of His handiwork, and as stewards, we are called to honor and preserve this intricate tapestry. Sadly, throughout history, humanity has often failed in its stewardship. We have exploited and neglected the earth, causing harm to both the environment and mankind. We have succumbed to greed, selfishness, and a shortsighted perspective that fails to consider the long-term consequences of our actions. As a result, we witness the devastating effects of pollution, deforestation, climate change, and the exploitation of natural resources.

However, as believers, we are called to a higher standard. We are called to reclaim our role as responsible stewards and agents of God's restoration. This begins with recognizing our dominion is not absolute but subservient to the sovereignty of our Creator. We are to exercise our authority in harmony with His divine will and purposes. To fulfill our role as faithful stewards, we must adopt an attitude of humility and gratitude. We must cultivate a deep reverence for God's creation and seek to understand its interconnectedness. We should strive to be mindful of the impact of our choices and actions, considering the well-being of future generations. We are called to be agents of healing, restoration, and justice in a broken world.

As we reflect on Psalm 8:6, let us remember the magnitude of our calling as stewards of God's creation. May we approach this responsibility with humility, seeking wisdom and guidance from our Heavenly Father. May our actions reflect our gratitude for the beauty and abundance that surrounds us. Let us embrace the task of caring for the earth and its inhabitants, knowing our faithful stewardship brings honor to the One who entrusted it to us.

Changed

Day 77 Exercises

1. What changes should be made in your life now that you realize God created you to rule for Him?

___

2. Knowing God values you above all else, what will change about your life?

___

3. Why did God choose to place all things under your feet?

___

4. In what ways have you failed to be a good steward of God's gifts to you and how will you do better?

___

Week 12

> *"Passing the test and giving the testimony, not failing the test and having the moanies."*

The end of the matter is eternity. Everyone will find an eternity in one of two places, Heaven or Hell. Heaven is the eternal dwelling place of God, and it is described a realm of unimaginable beauty, joy, and perfection. Hell is a place completely separated from God and is described as a place of fiery torment, where there will be pain, suffering, weeping and gnashing of teeth. As believers, we are privileged to have the hope of spending eternity in the glorious realm of Heaven. However, it is not a gift to be kept to ourselves; it is a gift meant to be shared. By embracing the wonders of Heaven and diligently seeking to help others find salvation, we participate in God's redemptive plan and become vessels of His love and grace. Let us explore the magnificence of Heaven and the urgency of bringing others into its eternal blessings.

Heaven is beyond our limited human comprehension. It is a place where pain, sorrow, and sin cease to exist. In Heaven we will behold the face of God, experience perfect fellowship with Him, and bask in the fullness of His Glory. It is a realm of unending joy, where tears are wiped away, and every longing of our hearts finds complete fulfillment. The beauty of Heaven surpasses all earthly splendors, for it is a place of eternal peace, righteousness, and love. Meditating on the wonders of Heaven fills our hearts with awe and gratitude, igniting a passion within us to share this incredible hope with others.

Recognizing the glories of Heaven highlights the urgency of salvation. As we witness the brokenness and pain in the world, we realize the desperate need for the redemptive work of Christ. Every soul is precious in the sight of God, and His desire is that none should perish. The reality of eternity without God should compel us to reach out to the lost, for in their salvation, they will partake in the eternal blessings of Heaven. We are called to be ambassadors of Christ, proclaiming the message of salvation and extending a lifeline of hope to those who are lost and in despair.

Helping others find salvation involves more than preaching with words; it requires demonstrating God's love through our actions. By displaying compassion, kindness, and selflessness, we reflect the character of Christ and draw people closer to Him. Our love and genuine concern for others are tangible expressions of God's grace and mercy. As we actively engage in acts of service, ministering to the needs of the hurting and marginalized, we demonstrate the Gospel's transformative power. Through our love, others can catch a glimpse of the Heavenly realm and the depth of God's love for them.

Changed

Sharing the gift of salvation is a sacred privilege. We are called to proclaim the Good News boldly, for it is the power of God unto salvation. Through our testimonies, we share how God's grace has transformed our lives, offering hope and redemption to those who are lost. Our words carry the potential to ignite faith, inspire repentance, and lead others to accept Jesus as their Lord and Savior. We must be intentional in our evangelism, seizing opportunities to share the message of salvation and inviting others into a personal relationship with Christ.

The glories of Heaven await us, but they are not meant for us alone. As we grasp the magnificence of this eternal realm, our hearts are stirred to share the gift of salvation with others. Let us recognize the urgency of salvation and actively engage in bringing the lost into the embrace of God's love. Through our words, actions, and genuine care for others, we become instruments of God's grace, pointing people towards the eternal joys of Heaven. May we fervently seek to help others find salvation so that they may experience the indescribable glories of eternity with our loving Heavenly Father.

DAY 78

HELPING HANDS

> *Galatians 6:1-2*
>
> *"¹ Brothers and sisters, if someone is caught in a sin, you who live by the Spirit should restore that person gently. But watch yourselves, or you also may be tempted. ² Carry each other's burdens, and in this way you will fulfill the law of Christ."*

We are reminded in today's passage that the flesh nature, sin, does not simply disappear once we are born again. Salvation is instantaneous upon answering the call and surrendering our lives to Christ. The moment we receive the Holy Spirit we are transformed from death to life, from rejected to accepted, and from bound to free. At that moment, God changes us, the old man is dead and we are made new through Him. The transformation is instantaneous but becoming a mature believer is a process that will continue throughout our lives.

Relationships are either growing and developing or they are falling apart. The same is true with our relationship with God. It is either developing or dying. There is no plateau. As a Christian we should always be seeking to know God more and striving to be more like Him. That is the maturing process. As long as we are striving, we are right where we are supposed to be, transformed but not yet fully perfected. The day we enter our eternal reward in Heaven is the day the work will be done, completed, and perfected.

Saved, born-again, transformed, and free believers are no longer slaves to sin. The flesh nature can no longer dictate what they do or how they live. Sin no longer has control over them. If a believer is still struggling with sin and feeding the flesh nature, it is because they have chosen to do so. When Christ sets an individual free, the only way sin can capture them again is if they allow it. Somewhere, somehow they have made a conscious choice to stop seeking the Lord.

Sin is simply the byproduct of a distant relationship with God. The truth is, everything we do affects our relationship with the Lord and our relationship with the Lord affects everything we do. The closer our walk with God is, the more transformed we are and the less we struggle with sin. The more strained our relationship with the Lord is, the more we will find ourselves actively feeding the flesh nature and sinning. Today's verse not only reminds us of our own propensity to sin but instructs us to gently "restore" fellow believers that may be participating in sinful ways. We should understand that every one of us are sinners, saved by grace and anyone of us are potentially only a few bad choices away from being a believer "caught in sin."

Gently restoring a fellow believer means we don't stand in judgment, we don't view ourselves as being better than them, nor do we condemn the person. We can condemn the sin, but not the person. We are told to "carry each other's burdens," which means we are called to help that person reject whatever sin they have been caught in. Repentance begins when we admit our shortcomings to God, reject them, and stop making excuses for them. Our prayers and support, as well as Godly counsel and instruction can help someone caught in sin to escape. Our love can change everything. After all, James 5:19-20 states: "My brothers and sisters, if one of you should wander from the truth and someone should bring that person back, remember this: Whoever turns a sinner from the error of their way will save them from death and cover over a multitude of sins."

Changed

Day 78 Exercises

1. How can I ensure that I won't fall back into old sinful habits?

2. In what ways can I gently restore a fellow believer who is struggling?

3. What does it mean to you that our relationship with the Lord affects everything we do?

4. What does it mean to you that sin is a choice?

DAY 79

ETERNAL LIFE

> *John 5:24*
>
> *"Very truly I tell you, whoever hears my word and believes him who sent me has eternal life and will not be judged but has crossed over from death to life."*

Today, we start our reading with the words of Christ, "Very truly I tell you." These words should grab our attention just as they did for those who heard them when Jesus first spoke them. These words were spoken to grab the attention of those listening and they are there to grab our attention as well. Jesus is conveying that what He is about to tell them is crucial and they should pay close attention. Jesus goes on to state, "Whoever hears my word and believes Him who sent Me has eternal life." It is this passage that Jesus declares the path upon which we have eternal security and assurance of Salvation.

Eternal security is the truth that once we are His we don't need to fear being rejected. We don't have to live in fear, thinking that at any moment we may do something that will cause Him to stop loving us. While we know sin separates us from Him and if we are unrepentant we will not find eternal life. Eternal security lets us know His love transcends our shortcomings. This is not a freedom to live a life of sin once we claim to know Him, because if we can do that then we have never truly given our lives to Him. The truth is, once we have seen and tasted how good the Lord is, there is no going back. We will never be satisfied until we are back in a right relationship with Him.

The external assurance of Salvation comes only by hearing and believing. I won't get into the word "believe" again as we have already discussed its truths. Simply put, it is not just knowing but is also acting. The word "hearing" used here is also not merely the passive act of listening. In order to have the eternal assurance we desire we must be listening actively. Our listening should be through a transformative engagement with God's Word. As we immerse ourselves in Scripture and its truths penetrate our hearts, our faith grows deeper and deeper and our actions follow. "Hearing" and "believing" moves past a head-knowledge and goes straight to the heart. Not only do we know that we need Jesus, but we also become willing to surrender and trust Him for all of our life. The great news for us is that our passage doesn't stop there. It goes even deeper. Jesus goes on to declare that by hearing and believing, we will not be judged. This is the assurance we have through Christ, the assurance that our sins, mistakes, and shortcomings will not be judged because of our faith in Him. Jesus paid the penalty for our sin. When we accept Him, we do not receive the death sentence we deserve but instead get eternal life.

For those who have placed their faith in Him, there is no looming judgment, no impending condemnation. Instead, there is freedom – freedom from guilt, shame, and the power of sin and death. This spiritual transformation is a divine change that we receive by faith through grace. It is when we begin the journey from darkness into light, despair into hope, and spiritual death into abundant life. Fear is replaced by faith, bondage turned to freedom, and misery becomes victory. We are changed from those condemned to death into those who have eternal life. In Christ, we find that the hope of eternal security is all we need for our present sustenance. Today's verse is a promise upon which we can stand, knowing His grace is sufficient for each moment and we are free from judgment and condemnation.

Changed

Day 79 Exercises

1. Explain eternal security as you understand it.

2. Can you live how you want and still go to Heaven?

3. Explain how you can bypass judgment.

4. Describe the ways in which you are or are not hearing and believing.

DAY 80
ETERNITY

> *Matthew 25:46*
>
> *"Then they will go away to eternal punishment, but the righteous to eternal life."*

Today, we read Jesus' words that should stir our hearts and awaken our souls to the reality of eternity. Jesus reveals the destiny that awaits each and every one of us. We can see there are two possible outcomes for eternity and that our eternal destination hinges on a crucial choice. Our choice encompasses more than just the right here and right now, because our choices will determine our eternity. These words of Jesus here should compel us to reflect on our lives and consider the weight of our decisions. Understanding this should cause us to be careful as our choices hold the power to shape our eternal destiny.

Jesus shares that eternity is divided between two possible outcomes: eternal punishment and eternal life. He clearly distinguishes between those who choose to follow Him, the righteous, and those who reject Him. These words are a solemn reminder that our choices matter. Everything we choose has consequences, and many of those choices have eternal consequences. We must understand God desires all people to experience eternal life. There are none He chooses to condemn. Instead, He extends His grace, mercy, and love to everyone. Even more, He gives the free gift of salvation through faith in Jesus Christ. God condemns no one, but those who are condemned have condemned themselves through their rejection of God's Son. Today, we are reminded the choice is ultimately ours. It lies within our hands. We must personally respond to God's invitation and choose to accept or reject the salvation He freely offers.

The weightiness of this choice should guide us to ensure we know beyond any doubt that we have acknowledged Jesus as our Lord and Savior. Are we accepting His forgiveness and allowing His transformative power to shape our lives or have we chosen to avoid His grace and mercy, seeking our own path? The consequences are real. Rejecting God's offer of salvation, Jesus, will bring about eternal punishment. We cannot dismiss this, ignore it, or think it isn't true just because we deny it. Truth is truth regardless of what we may personally believe, and the truth is, we will all have an eternity. Those who have accepted Christ as their Savior will have eternal life, and those who reject Him will have eternal punishment. God, being just and righteous, cannot tolerate sin, and those who persist in rebellion against Him will face the consequences of their actions.

However, this verse serves as a message of hope and promise for those who will receive Him. Jesus affirms the righteous will inherit eternal life. This eternal life is not merely an extension of our earthly existence but a glorious and unending union with our Creator, filled with joy, peace, and perfect communion with Him. The righteous are not those who achieve perfection or earn their salvation through their own efforts but rather those who have placed their trust in the finished work of Jesus on the cross. Through His sacrifice, we are made righteous before God, and through faith in Him, we receive the gift of eternal life with Him.

We should consider the brevity of our earthly lives and the weight of our choices. We need to be called to action, examine our hearts, repent of our sins, and turn to Jesus as the only way to eternal life. Let God ignite a passion within you to live for His Kingdom and to be an ambassador of His grace and love.

Changed

Day 80 Exercises

1. Have you accepted Jesus as your Lord and Savior, if so how do you know?

_____
_____
_____
_____
_____
_____
_____

2. Explain the contrast of eternity for those who are saved and those who have rejected Salvation.

_____
_____
_____
_____
_____
_____
_____
_____
_____

3. What assurance do the righteous have of an eternal reward?

_____
_____
_____
_____
_____
_____
_____
_____

4. Explain how any one of us can be righteous.

_____
_____
_____
_____
_____
_____
_____

DAY 81

DISPLAYED

> *Matthew 10:26*
>
> *"So do not be afraid of them, for there is nothing concealed that will not be disclosed, or hidden that will not be made known."*

There is nothing hidden that will not be made known. Today's verse will probably bring both encouragement and concern in equal amounts. We should all stand encouraged that God sees and knows all. He knows the things that bring anxiety and fear into our lives. He knows the things done to us by those who oppose us, the things done, secretly and publicly. Our verse today assures us that all those things hidden will be uncovered, and the truth will be revealed. Whatever is done to us, God sees and knows it, and regardless of what others may have intended, God can bring forth His plan.

The first part of our passage today begins with Jesus proclaiming: "Have no fear of them..." God knows how fear can cripple us. God knows that fear will rob us of our joy and peace and prevent us from walking in His plan for our lives. Fearing "them" is to have a fear of others, their opinion of us, or their position over us.

God simply reminds us we do not need to fear anyone other than Him. We are to abandon fear and instead embrace faith. No matter how dark the world around us may be or how much we may be filled with uncertainties, we can take comfort in the knowledge God sees it all and knows it all. Nothing can remain concealed from His sight. When we trust in His divine timing, we can release our fears and rest assured God's truth will prevail.

The fact that nothing is hidden also brings concern because God sees all we do. He knows our hearts, and we can't hide anything from Him. We may be able to fool others or even ourselves, but we can't fool God. He unmasks all hidden thing. As Jesus said: "...for nothing is covered that will not be revealed, or hidden that will not be made known."

This means the truth will prevail. The truth will break through every fortified barrier. No matter how hard people try to conceal their actions or motives, their efforts are ultimately futile in the face of God's sovereignty. As believers we can take heart, knowing the truth will always prevail. In time, all hidden things will be brought to light, exposing falsehood and the pure essence of God's truth.

We would do well to remember God's timing and justice will prevail. Injustice will not go unpunished, for His timing and justice are perfect. As we face trials and witness injustice, we can find solace in knowing since God sees all things, one day, every wrong will be made right.

Matthew 10:26 reminds us to release our fears and trust God's sovereignty. We are to take comfort in knowing the truth will always prevail and darkness will be exposed. As we navigate a world filled with uncertainty and opposition, may we hold fast to our faith.

Changed

Day 81 Exercises

1. What have you been hiding from God?

2. How has God revealed those things you have hidden?

3. What things have been done to you that have been hidden?

4. Explain the comfort you find in knowing that all those hidden things done to you will be made known.

DAY 82
MANSION

> *John 14:2*
>
> *"My Father's house has many rooms; if that were not so, would I have told you that I am going there to prepare a place for you?"*

In our verse today, Jesus makes several declarations. When Jesus says that He is "going there to prepare a place for you," He professes He can actually prepare a place for those who have trusted in Him and been born again. This "going" the Lord is stating He will do is Him declaring He will soon be physically absent from this world. He is sharing with us that His physical absence from the earth will not be because someone has done away with Him. In fact, the Lord is stating His departure is of His own free will. It is an intentional decision, as He has an assignment to complete; the preparation of an eternal home for us.

We know He is referencing Heaven as He declares He is going to His Father's house to prepare a place for us. We can look back at Matthew 6 when Jesus states we are to pray to "Our Father, who art in Heaven." Then, in 1 Kings 22:19, it states: "Micaiah said, "Therefore, hear the word of the Lord. I saw the Lord sitting on His throne, and all the host of Heaven standing by Him on His right and on His left." There are many more references to the Father being in Heaven and Jesus being at His right hand. This makes it easy for us to conclude the place Jesus is going is Heaven, and the place we have is Heavenly.

The portion of Scripture that declares there are many rooms there is exciting to me, as it signifies there is room for each of us. The space is not lacking; we won't have to fight for a spot, nor will we be on the outside looking in. The fact there are many rooms simply means every room needed will be available. This means there is room for you if you have been born again. It isn't a matter of how much you know, how much you have accomplished, or even how perfect you are. It simply matters if you are His.

Many religions teach salvation by works, but this isn't what the Bible teaches. The Bible is clear that we are all sinners, we all fall short, and none of us will ever be righteous on our own. The Bible declares God's grace saves us through our faith in Him. We simply need to receive the Lord and allow His righteousness to be imputed to us, since He is the only righteous One. If and when we do this, we can be assured Heaven has reserved a place for us.

Accepting this truth has changed everything for me. For years, after giving my life to Christ, I felt like I needed to structure my life in such a way that He could accept me. I would read specific amounts of Scriptures each day, fast, pray, and avoid anything that might have even the appearance of sin. Living like that was exhausting, unrealistic, and offensive to God. It took a lot to have this religious spirit broken in my life, but by God breaking me down, I realized that the best I could accomplish for God was still revolting to Him.

I learned to accept the fact that God loves me regardless and the things He doesn't feel should be a part of my life, He will fix. I learned it was never my responsibility to fix me, but only my responsibility to allow Him to reconcile me to whom He created me to be in the first place.

Changed

Day 82 Exercises

1. Is the Lord preparing a place for you? Why, or why not?

2. How do you feel about it being your responsibility to allow God to change you?

3. How are you going to allow God to complete the work He has begun in you?

4. Describe yourself and your life just how God designed it?

DAY 83

SEPARATED

> *Matthew 25:31-32*
>
> *"³¹ When the Son of Man comes in his glory, and all the angels with him, he will sit on his glorious throne. ³² All the nations will be gathered before him, and he will separate the people one from another as a shepherd separates the sheep from the goats."*

The day described above is coming, and as believers, the anticipation of Jesus taking His rightful place in all His Glory should bring great excitement. It's hard to imagine how amazing it will be when a multitude of angels accompanies Jesus, and we are there before Him, in His Divine presence, seeing every knee bow before Him. It won't matter the nationality, race, or religion. All people, young, old, black, white, atheist or believer, will bow before Him, and all will recognize His authority. Then, the most wonderful and tragic moment of all eternity will occur. Before His splendor, as all the nations gather, He will separate those born again from those not. The passage today is a reminder of what is to come. It verifies the King will return one day to judge the living and the dead. At that moment it will be too late to change the eternal consequences of your life and the choices you have made. There, kneeling before His Glory, many will beg and plead for one more chance, but none will be given. We must choose today. We must choose now, while we are still present on this earth, while He is still drawing us towards repentance. Choosing Jesus as Lord and Savior is not a decision we should wait to make. It is not something we can put off until we are ready.

The Bible says He chooses us, not that we choose Him. This means when He calls, we need to answer. The idea of living our lives independently from Him and waiting until we are old and done before we reach out to Him isn't Scriptural, and it won't work. In today's passage, Jesus compares Himself to a shepherd separating the sheep from the goats. It was common in Biblical times for shepherds to lead their flocks of sheep and goats together during the day, but at night, they would separate them. This is a description of humanity. While it is still day, so to speak, the sheep and the goats are living together, but there is coming a time when Christ Himself will distinguish those who belong to Him and those who don't. This separation won't be based on external appearances or worldly achievements. It won't be determined by the clothes we wear, the social status we hold, or the possessions we accumulate. It will be based on the condition of our hearts and our relationship with Him. The sheep represent the righteous, those who have responded to Jesus' invitation to follow Him. They have placed their faith in Him, allowing His love and grace to transform their lives. Their lives have been a witness to their faith, and they lived in accordance with the fruit of the Spirit described in Galatians 5:22-23. The goats represent the unrighteous, those who have rejected or neglected the call of Jesus. They have been indifferent to the needs of others, acted selfishly, had a lack of compassion, and disregarded Biblical values.

The separation itself serves as a great reminder that a deep, personal relationship with Jesus is vital. Our faith must be genuine and transformative, not merely lip service or religious observance. Just going through the motions won't allow you to make the cut. Remember, Jesus sees the heart, and He knows all. Living with lip service and no real dedication may fool all those around you. You may even fool yourself, but the Lord knows His own and He sees the heart. We should ask ourselves whether we live as sheep or goats. Are we faithfully following the Shepherd, bearing the fruit of righteousness, or are we wandering aimlessly, consumed by our own desires and self-centeredness? Remember, the passage today is a warning of what is to come. We will kneel before the King of Kings, and He will separate us. We must strive to live our lives to honor Him, seeking to love and serve others with the love and grace we have received from Him.

Changed

Day 83 Exercises

1. Describe the difference between sheep and goats in reference to our passage.

2. Based on your understanding, which are you, a sheep or a goat? Why?

3. Explain the eternal resting place of both the sheep and the goats.

4. What needs to take place in your life and what must change for you to be considered one of His sheep?

DAY 84

LUKEWARM

> *Revelation 3:16*
>
> *"So, because you are lukewarm, neither hot nor cold, I am about to spit you out of my mouth."*

In our passage today, Jesus addresses the church in Laodicea with a message that still applies today. His words are meant as a warning to all who belong to Him not to be lukewarm. Being lukewarm is a very dangerous place to be. If you remember, as in all relationships, our relationship with God is either growing or dying. Becoming lukewarm is where we are comfortable, neither fully committed nor fully indifferent.

Spiritually, it is a dangerous place to be because it fosters complacency and self-reliance. Jesus' words are a wake-up call to remind us half-hearted devotion is unacceptable in His Kingdom. We need to understand the severity of Jesus saying: "I am about to spit you out of my mouth." Some translations use the word vomit to describe just how untasteful to God a lukewarm relationship is. We must realize God expects wholehearted devotion from His followers. He wants us to be passionate about our faith, fervent in our love for Him, and committed to living out His teachings.

The Laodiceans thought they had it all together. They thought since their lives were "blessed," God was pleased with them. Instead of trusting in the Lord and depending on Him, they became dependent on their material wealth and self-sufficiency. We must remember those who suffer are not always suffering because they are wrong with God and those who are blessed are not always right with God. The scripture states in Matthew 5:45 "...He causes His sun to rise on the evil and the good, and sends rain on the righteous and the unrighteous." This means the just and unjust both may get just what they need. Having a good job, good house or a good anything is not a gauge of a right relationship with God.

The Laodiceans put on a good outward show. They had all the right things to say and do, but God saw through the show. He sees the heart and He knows us. Too often we gauge success on outward appearances. God judges the heart and He knows that it is easy to appear outwardly successful yet be spiritually bankrupt. The Laodiceans lacked the one thing that truly mattered: a vibrant, intimate relationship with their Lord and Savior. God does not honor half-hearted commitment. He knows Spiritual complacency will destroy us. We can't just go through the motions; we must fully engage our heart, mind, body, and soul. We can't prioritize worldly pursuits over our relationship with God.

Lukewarmness is more dangerous than being fully hot or fully cold. It puts us in a state where we believe we're fine and don't need to change. Those fully cold know they need Jesus, they know they need help, and they know they need to change to be right. The problem is, those lukewarm are in the same spiritually bankrupt situation as those who are cold but they don't even know it. The lukewarm are on the verge of being rejected but think God is pleased with them. That is an awful place to be, to feel right but be wrong. We must not deceive ourselves. The only acceptable relationship with God is one that is fully dedicated to Him. God loves us and wants each of us to be with Him for eternity. If you've been cold or lukewarm, repent and get right with Him.

Changed

Day 84 Exercises

1. Describe a lukewarm lifestyle.

2. Why is being lukewarm so dangerous?

3. In what ways have you been lukewarm?

4. Describe a lifestyle that is hot and right with God.

Week 13

"Walk-talk, not talk-talk"

We have our walk-talk and our talk-talk, but our walk-talk speaks way louder than our talk-talk. This is why it is so important for us to live out our beliefs for all to see. In seeing us live the way He designed, others will be encouraged to do the same.

As followers of Christ, we are called to live victoriously, overcoming the challenges, trials, and temptations that come our way. This victorious life is not based on our own strengths or abilities but on our unwavering trust in God's power and the promises He has given us. Through faith, obedience, and a deep relationship with Him, we can experience triumph over sin, fear, and the schemes of the enemy. Let us explore the keys to living victoriously and embracing the abundant life God has designed for us.

Living victoriously begins with surrendering our lives completely to God. It is acknowledging that apart from Him, we are powerless, but with Him, all things are possible. In surrendering, we release our own desires, plans, and control; allowing God to work in and through us. It is in our surrender that we find true strength. We depend on God for wisdom, guidance, and the power to overcome. As we submit ourselves to Him daily, we invite His Spirit to empower us and lead us into victorious living.

God's Word is a powerful weapon that equips us for victorious living. It is a source of wisdom, encouragement, and truth. By immersing ourselves in Scripture, we gain a deeper understanding of God's character, His promises, and His will for our lives. His Word provides guidance in making the right choices, strength in times of weakness, and hope in the face of adversity. Meditating on and applying God's Word enables us to stand firm against the schemes of the enemy and overcome the trials that come our way.

Living victoriously requires unwavering faith and trust in God. It is believing that He is always with us, working all things for our good. When we encounter challenges and uncertainties, we trust that God is in control and that His plans are perfect. Our faith allows us to step out of our comfort zones, pursue God-given dreams and visions, and embrace the opportunities He presents to us. As we trust in His provision, guidance, and timing, we experience the joy of seeing His faithfulness unfold in our lives.

Prayer and worship are essential aspects of living victoriously. We commune with God through prayer, expressing our needs, concerns, and praises. In prayer, we lay our burdens before Him and seek His strength and guidance. Worship, on the other hand, redirects our focus from ourselves to the greatness of God. It reminds us of His sovereignty, goodness, and faithfulness.

Changed

In the presence of God, we find comfort, peace, and renewed strength. Both prayer and worship deepen our intimacy with God and position us to receive His power and grace to live victoriously. Living victoriously is not an easy path, but it is a journey filled with God's presence, power, and promises. As we surrender ourselves to Him, cling to His Word, walk in faith, and engage in prayer and worship, we tap into the abundant life that Jesus came to give us. The challenges we face are opportunities for God to display His strength and for us to experience His victory. Let us embrace the victorious life God offers, knowing that through Him, we can conquer any obstacle and live a life that brings glory to His Name.

DAY 85
TRUE LOVE

> *John 3:16-18*
>
> *"16 For God so loved the world that he gave his one and only Son, that whoever believes in him shall not perish but have eternal life. 17 For God did not send his Son into the world to condemn the world, but to save the world through him. 18 Whoever believes in him is not condemned, but whoever does not believe stands condemned already because they have not believed in the name of God's one and only Son."*

Today's passage may be one of the most quoted Scriptures. These verses capture the essence of God's love and the incredible gift of salvation He has provided. Jesus spoke these words during His conversation with Nicodemus, and they illustrate God's profound love for us and His gift to us through Christ. The love described here is not for just you and me but for all of humanity. God truly loves each of us and has provided a way that none of us should perish but all find everlasting life.

"For God so loved the world." These simple words reveal the very heart of God and the magnitude of His love. His love truly surpasses all of our understanding. He extends this love to the righteous, broken, lost, and undeserving. God's love is a love that transcends boundaries, cultures, and generations. His love is boundless and all-encompassing, reaching out to every corner of the world and every corner of our hearts. The words that state: "He gave his one and only Son," declare God's love was not merely a sentiment or an emotion but an action. Out of His boundless love, God gave the most precious gift imaginable, His Son, Jesus Christ. When you think about what happened for God to express His love, it is truly amazing. Jesus, God incarnated in the flesh, left all the splendor and Glory of Heaven to live with us. He came to teach us, heal us, and ultimately offer Himself as the perfect, sinless sacrifice for our sins. This is how much God loves us. He willingly stepped down from Glory to give Himself as a Holy sacrifice for us who are not deserving.

The above Scripture declares, "Whoever believes in him shall not perish but have eternal life." The gift of salvation is offered to all who believe in Jesus Christ. This is more than just believing He existed or even just believing He is the Son of God who gave His life as a payment for our sins. When we really believe in and accept Him as our Lord and Savior, we declare: He rules our lives, He is over all that we do, and we are subject to Him. In this, we are delivered from the consequences of our sins and granted eternal life in the presence of God. Verse 17, above reads: "For God did not send his Son into the world to condemn the world, but to save the world through him." God's ultimate purpose for sending Jesus was not to condemn any of us to Hell. His purpose in sending Jesus was to save us. It is our own sinful ways that have already left us condemned and separated from God. Yet, God provided a way for reconciliation through His mercy and love. Through Jesus' sacrificial death and resurrection, He made a way for us to be reconciled to God and to experience the fullness of His love and salvation. "Whoever believes in him is not condemned, but whoever does not believe stands condemned already because they have not believed in the name of God's one and only Son." This verse highlights the fact that we each have a critical choice to make.—to believe in Jesus or to reject Him. Our response to this question determines our eternal destiny. Those who place their faith in Him are set free from condemnation and enter into a personal relationship with God. However, those who refuse to believe will remain in a state of condemnation, separated from the love and grace of God.

Day 85 Exercises

1. What does being condemned mean?

2. Describe who and what a believer is.

3. Explain why you are or are not a believer.

4. Describe the love that God has for you.

DAY 86
GIFT OF GOD

> *Romans 6:23*
>
> *"For the wages of sin is death, but the gift of God is eternal life in Christ Jesus our Lord."*

In today's verse, Romans 6:23, the apostle Paul presents us with a profound truth that gets to the core message of the Gospel. Within this verse, we find both the problem and the solution to humanity's greatest need: deliverance from sin. "The wages of sin is death." This declaration confronts us with the reality of sin's consequences.

Sin is not a mere mistake or a minor indiscretion but a rebellion against God's perfect and holy standards. Sin separates us from our Creator and brings forth physical and spiritual death. The wages, what we earn for our sin, the rightful payment, so to speak, is death and eternal separation from God. Our sinfulness taints our souls and renders us incapable of bridging the gap between us and our Creator. No amount of human effort or good works can undo the devastating consequences of sin.

The Good News is that our verse does not end there; it offers us hope as it proclaims, "But the gift of God is eternal life in Christ Jesus our Lord." Despite our sinful nature and the death that awaits us for it, God has extended an extraordinary gift of love to all who believe in His Son, Jesus Christ. The gift of eternal life is the exact opposite of the death we deserve. Eternal life is an undeserved, unearned, and unmerited gift from a gracious and loving God.

The best part is that it is not based on our own abilities, work, or worthiness. It is entirely a manifestation of God's boundless love and mercy towards humanity. It is a gift that transcends the limitations of our earthly existence, offering us a restored relationship with our Creator and the promise of life everlasting. In Christ Jesus, we find redemption, forgiveness, and hope for a future that extends far beyond this temporary world. To fully appreciate the magnitude of this gift, we must recognize the cost that was paid on our behalf. Jesus, the sinless Son of God, willingly took the weight of our sins upon Himself. He suffered and died on the cross, bearing the punishment that we deserved. His sacrificial act became the bridge that spans the gap between a Holy God and sinful humanity. Through His resurrection, He conquered sin and death, offering us the hope of eternal life.

The gift of eternal life is given to us freely, but it cost God everything. This gift demands a response from us. We are called to acknowledge our need for Jesus as our Savior. We must repent of our sins and place our faith and trust in Jesus Christ. We must surrender our lives to Him, allowing His grace to transform us from the inside out. What we receive is not merely a ticket to Heaven but a new way to live that is connected to God and fellow believers. This new life compels us to walk in obedience, pursue righteousness, and share the Good News of salvation with a world in desperate need.

As we meditate on all of this, may we be filled with gratitude for God's unimaginable grace and respond to His invitation wholeheartedly. May the truth of this verse permeate every aspect of our lives, shaping our choices, priorities, and interactions. And may we continually reflect the love and mercy of our Savior, extending His invitation of eternal life to all who are lost and in need of redemption.

Changed

Day 86 Exercises

1. Explain today's Scripture in your own words.

2. Is a gift based on the giver or the receiver and why does this matter?

3. Why are we offered eternal life through Jesus?

4. What must you do to receive the gift of eternal life?

DAY 87

POWER

> *Ephesians 1:19-21*
>
> *"19 and his incomparably great power for us who believe. That power is the same as the mighty strength 20 he exerted when he raised Christ from the dead and seated him at his right hand in the Heavenly realms, 21 far above all rule and authority, power and dominion, and every name that is invoked, not only in the present age but also in the one to come."*

In Ephesians 1:19-21, the apostle Paul invites us to grasp the incomparable greatness of God's power. He shares that this power is available to each of us who are His children. The power described here exceeds all human understanding and is intimately connected to the resurrection and exaltation of Jesus Christ. As we meditate on these verses, let us open our hearts to comprehend the limitless power and authority we have been given through our Lord Jesus Christ.

The passage begins with Paul's prayer for the Ephesian believers and all Christ's followers throughout the ages. He desires that we understand and fully embrace the magnitude of God's power that is at work within us. Paul is determined to make sure we know this power is not distant or inaccessible but that it is a power that is intimately connected to our faith in God. As we believe in God and surrender our lives to His will, His power is unleashed in and through us. This power is the same mighty power that raised Christ from the dead. It is a power that overcomes the forces of sin and death, triumphing over every obstacle which stands in the way. Through His resurrection, Jesus demonstrated His authority over all things and secured our victory over sin and the enemy. This resurrection power is not limited to a one-time event in history but is available to each of us today. This life-transforming power is being poured into our lives, and it is enabling us to live victoriously.

Furthermore, this power elevated Christ to the place of highest honor at God's right hand in the Heavenly realms and placed all things under His feet. Because of this power, He is reigning over all creation, with all authority, and He has surpassed every ruler, authority, power, or leader, not only in this world but also in the world to come. This position of supremacy gives us confidence and assurance that nothing can overpower or overshadow the authority of our Lord. As believers, we are not left powerless or defenseless in this world. We have been granted access to the same divine power that resurrected Christ and exalted Him to the highest place. This power is available to us through the indwelling of the Holy Spirit. The Holy Spirit empowers and equips us to live out our faith, overcome challenges, and fulfill God's purposes in our lives.

Understanding and experiencing this power transforms our perspective on life's circumstances. When we face trials, we can draw strength from the knowledge that the same power that conquered death resides within us. When we encounter spiritual opposition, we can stand firm in the authority of Christ, knowing He has already overcome every spiritual force. This power enables us to walk in victory, resist temptation, love sacrificially, and impact the world around us with the transformative message of the Gospel. We shouldn't underestimate or overlook the incredible greatness of God's power that is available to us. It is a power that far surpasses anything we can imagine or comprehend. As we deepen our relationship with God and grow in our understanding of His power, let us continually rely on His strength and seek to align our lives with His purposes. Let us surrender our own limitations and allow His power to work through us, bringing about transformation in our lives and in the lives of others.

Changed

Day 87 Exercises

1. Describe the power spoken about in today's passage and where it comes from.

_____
_____
_____
_____
_____
_____
_____
_____

2. How do you have access to this power and how do you obtain it?

_____
_____
_____
_____
_____
_____
_____
_____
_____
_____

3. Describe what God's power can accomplish in your life.

_____
_____
_____
_____
_____
_____
_____
_____

4. What does it mean for you to have the same power that raised Christ from the dead living in you?

_____
_____
_____
_____
_____
_____
_____
_____

DAY 88

FRUIT

> *Galatians 5:22-23*
>
> *"²² But the fruit of the Spirit is love, joy, peace, forbearance, kindness, goodness, faithfulness, ²³ gentleness and self-control. Against such things there is no law."*

In the book of Galatians, the apostle Paul emphasizes the importance of living a life led by the Spirit rather than by the desires of the flesh. Too many of us have way more experience living to please our fleshy desires. To combat this, Paul introduces us to the fruit of the Spirit. The fruit is what is produced by living a born-again, surrendered life to Christ. The fruit of the Spirit serves as a roadmap for us and identifies our transformation in Christ. The fruit of the Spirit reflects the character of God and bears witness to His work in our lives. Today, we will look at these specific fruits individually.

Love: Love is the pinnacle of Christian virtue. It embodies selflessness, compassion, and unconditional care for others. As we yield to the Holy Spirit, He enables us to love God with all our hearts and our neighbors as ourselves.

Joy: Joy is not dependent upon our circumstances but is a deep-seated gladness that flows from knowing God and His faithfulness. The Holy Spirit infuses our hearts with a supernatural joy that surpasses earthly happiness, allowing us to rejoice even amid trials.

Peace: The peace the Holy Spirit brings transcends all understanding. It is not merely the absence of conflict but a tranquility that stems from our trust in God's sovereignty. In times of chaos, the peace of God guards our hearts and minds, providing stability and assurance.

Forbearance: Forbearance, also known as patience, allows us to endure difficulties and persevere in the face of challenges. The Holy Spirit empowers us to extend grace and forgiveness to others, reflecting our Heavenly Father's patience and long-suffering nature.

Kindness: Kindness is a tangible expression of God's love through our actions and words. The Holy Spirit molds our hearts to be sensitive to the needs of others, prompting us to offer acts of encouragement and compassion.

Goodness: The fruit of goodness reflects moral excellence and integrity. As we yield to the Holy Spirit's work, He enables us to live upright lives that honor God and inspire others who witness Christ's transformative power within us.

Faithfulness: Faithfulness is demonstrated through our unwavering commitment to God and our steadfastness in fulfilling our responsibilities. The Holy Spirit empowers us to remain loyal and dedicated to our relationship with God, enabling us to persevere in the face of trials and temptations.

Gentleness: Gentleness reflects humility, patience, and a controlled response, even in the face of provocation. The Holy Spirit refines our character, enabling us to respond to others with the gentle nature of our Savior, Jesus Christ.

Self-Control: Self-control is the fruit that empowers us to resist temptations, overcome sinful desires, and make choices which honor God. We are granted the strength and discipline to align our actions with God's will through the Holy Spirit's presence within us.

As believers, the fruit of the Spirit are not optional accessories but an essential evidence of our faith. It is an outward manifestation of our inward transformation. When we surrender our lives to the Holy Spirit, allowing Him to work in us, the fruit He produces reflects the beauty of God's character in our lives.

Day 88 Exercises

1. Which fruits of the Spirit are lacking in your life?

2. Explain why you are lacking those specific fruit and what you can do to correct those deficiencies.

3. How does drawing closer to Jesus make you more like Him?

4. Which fruit of the Spirit can be easily seen by others in your life?

DAY 89

GRACE

> *Ephesians 2:8-9*
>
> *"⁸ For it is by grace you have been saved, through faith and this is not from yourselves, it is the gift of God ⁹ not by works, so that no one can boast."*

In our world, a person's achievements, accomplishments, and self-reliance often get noticed and admired. This is in actual contrast to the message of God's grace. In its simplistic explanation, God's grace is His unmerited favor toward us. Today's passage sums up the essence of the Gospel and reveals the foundational truth of our salvation. We are saved by grace alone, through faith alone, and it is entirely God's gift to us. It has nothing to do with our achievements, accomplishments or self-anything.

In our passage today, we can see that Paul emphasizes the essential nature of God's grace to salvation. He makes it clear we have been saved by grace, not as a result of our works. No amount of good deeds, moral uprightness, or religious rituals can earn us salvation. Eternal life truly is a gift freely given to us by a loving and merciful God. Understanding and embracing this truth is vital for our spiritual journey. It humbles us, reminding us that we are utterly dependent on God's grace for our salvation. Salvation is not a reward for our efforts but a demonstration of God's love and kindness to us.

Grace strips away any grounds for boasting or self-righteousness, allowing us to approach God with a spirit of humility and gratitude. The concept of grace challenges the human inclination to strive for self-justification. We often find ourselves trying to earn God's favor or believing we can somehow merit our salvation through our deeds. Yet, Scripture repeatedly tells us we fall short of God's perfect standard (Romans 3:23) and our righteousness is like filthy rags before Him (Isaiah 64:6). God's grace disrupts this futile cycle by declaring we are saved by grace through faith. In this context, faith refers to our response to God's grace. Our faith is to trust and rely on God to complete the work He has begun.

Our faith recognizes we are unable to save ourselves. Instead, we must place complete trust in the finished work of Christ on the cross. Paul clarifies that our faith is not of our own doing. In fact, our faith is also a gift from God. God initiates the process of salvation, drawing us to Himself and opening our hearts and minds to understand and respond to His grace. Our faith, then, becomes a response to the work of the Holy Spirit in our lives, not a result of our knowledge or strength.

By highlighting the unearned nature of salvation, Paul is declaring the all-encompassing role of God in our spiritual journey. Every step, from start to finish, manifests His grace. Our role is to receive the gift with gratitude, surrendering our lives to Him in acknowledgment of His sovereignty.

The knowledge that our salvation results from God's grace has profound implications for our relationship with Him. It assures us that our standing before God depends not on our performance but on His unwavering love and mercy. We no longer need to fear rejection or strive to perform. Instead, we can rest in the unchanging grace of God, knowing nothing can separate us from His love.

Changed

Day 89 Exercises

1. Explain God's grace and what it means for you.

2. How does understanding God's grace free you?

3. Is there anything you can do to earn God's grace? Why or why not?

4. Describe a life that is lived by faith in the Lord and that has been saved by grace.

DAY 90
RAISED TO LIFE

> *1 Thessalonians 4:16*
>
> *"For the Lord Himself will come down from Heaven, with a loud command, with the voice of the archangel and with the trumpet call of God, and the dead in Christ will rise first."*

As we come to the close of our time together in "90 Days to A New You," we would be amiss to finish without looking at the second coming of our Lord Jesus Christ. The Lord's return is a central theme throughout the Old and New Testaments. It is a glorious hope that has inspired and encouraged believers in every generation. In 1 Thessalonians 4:16, the apostle Paul unveils a breathtaking glimpse of this future event, igniting our hearts with anticipation and reminding us of the ultimate victory that awaits us.

Paul's words in this verse vividly describe the scene that will unfold when Jesus returns. It will be a moment of unparalleled power and majesty. The Lord Himself will descend from Heaven with a cry of command, signaling His authority over all creation. The voice of an archangel will resound, and the sound of the trumpet of God will fill the air, announcing the arrival of the King of Kings. This event marks the fulfillment of God's promise to gather His people to Himself and signals the consummation of His redemptive plan for humanity. The mention of the dead in Christ rising first emphasizes those who have died in faith will be united with Him in resurrection glory. What a glorious and awe-inspiring sight it will be! As we meditate on this passage, we are reminded of several essential truths that can profoundly impact our lives as believers.

The certainty of Christ's return: the Lord's return is not a mere possibility or a distant hope but a guaranteed promise. Jesus Himself declared that He would come again (John 14:3), and throughout the New Testament, we find numerous references to this blessed event. We can have full assurance that the One who conquered sin and death will return to gather His people and establish His eternal Kingdom. The hope that sustains us: the anticipation of Christ's return brings hope and encouragement to our daily lives. In a world often plagued by suffering, injustice, and uncertainty, we find solace in knowing one day Jesus will make everything right. This hope empowers us to persevere, stand firm in our faith, and live with an eternal perspective, knowing that our present trials are temporary, in stark contrast to the glory that awaits us.

The victory over death: the mention of the dead in Christ rising first reminds us that death has been conquered through Jesus' resurrection. As believers, we have the assurance that even physical death cannot separate us from the love of God. Just as Christ was raised to life, we too will experience the resurrection of our bodies and be reunited with our loved ones who have gone before us. This truth offers comfort and hope in the face of grief and loss. The urgency of readiness: knowing of Christ's return should prompt us to live lives of readiness and holiness. As Paul writes in 1 Thessalonians 5:6, we must be sober and watchful, aware of the times and seasons. We are called to be faithful stewards of the time, talents, and resources God has entrusted to us, always ready to meet our Savior face to face. Let us live each day with a sense of purpose, seeking to glorify Him in all we do.

As we contemplate 1 Thessalonians 4:16, let us embrace the glorious hope of Christ's return. May it ignite within us a passion to live for Him, to share the Good News of salvation, and to eagerly await His coming. Let us encourage one another with these words, spurring each other on to faithfulness and steadfastness in our journey of following Christ.

Changed

Day 90 Exercises

1. Explain Jesus' return and what it means for you.

_____
_____
_____
_____
_____
_____
_____
_____

2. How do you want to be living when the Lord comes back for His people?

_____
_____
_____
_____
_____
_____
_____
_____

3. What does Christ's return mean for the unbeliever?

_____
_____
_____
_____
_____
_____
_____
_____

4. Why should we be living with a sense of urgency?

_____
_____
_____
_____
_____
_____
_____
_____

Wrap Up
SPIRIT, NOT FLESH

> *John 3:6*
>
> *"That which is born of the flesh is flesh, and that which is born of the Spirit is spirit."*

Throughout this journey, we have been looking to understand our purpose and identity as victorious, born-again believers. We have seen that Christ, our Creator, has a unique and powerful plan for each of us. His plan is not hidden but laid out within the Scriptures, and He desires for us to: walk in it, embracing it all while aligning our lives with His teachings, developing our gifts, and cultivating a deep relationship with Him. As we close, I want to leave you with four areas that we all need to allow Christ to guide us in.

Acceptance and Surrender: Becoming who Christ created us to be starts with accepting who we are. We are fearfully and wonderfully made with unique talents, traits, and experiences. By surrendering our lives to Christ, we acknowledge His sovereignty and trust in His plan. Through prayer and reflection, we can continue to gain a deeper understanding of our purpose, discovering that our identity lies in being His beloved children. In accepting ourselves as God's creation, we find the freedom to embrace our true identity and live for the purpose for which we are created.

Renewing the Mind: To become who Christ created us to be, we must renew our minds daily. This involves aligning our thoughts with God's truth, as revealed in His Word. By meditating on Scripture, we replace negative self-perceptions with the knowledge that we are chosen, loved, and called for a divine purpose. As we immerse ourselves in God's promises, our perspectives shift, and we begin to see ourselves through His eyes. With a renewed mind, we can overcome self-doubt and walk confidently on the path set before us.

Cultivating Spiritual Gifts: Christ has bestowed unique gifts and talents upon each of us to serve His Kingdom. Recognizing and cultivating these gifts is essential to becoming who He created us to be. We can identify our talents and passions through prayer and seeking guidance from the Holy Spirit. As we invest time and effort in developing these gifts, we can use them to bless others, glorify God, and fulfill our purpose. Whether it be teaching, encouraging, serving, or creating, our gifts are a reflection of God's goodness and enable us to make a meaningful impact in the world.

Embracing Growth and Transformation: Becoming who Christ created us to be is not a static process, but rather, a journey of growth and transformation. Christ invites us to continually grow in our faith, character, and relationship with Him. Through the challenges, trials, and victories, we experience growth and become more like Him. As we embrace change and allow the Holy Spirit to work within us, we shed old patterns, attitudes, and behaviors that hinder our true identity. The process may sometimes be uncomfortable, but the result is a life reflecting Christ's love, grace, and truth. Becoming who Christ created us to be is a lifelong pursuit that requires intentionality, faith, and a deep connection with God. It involves accepting our uniqueness, renewing our minds, developing our gifts, and embracing growth and transformation. As we walk in alignment with God's plan, we find fulfillment, purpose, and a deep sense of belonging. I encourage you to continue this journey with courage, trusting God's promises are true and He will guide you every step of the way. Being who God created you to be brings honor to His Name and allows you to become a living testimony of His grace and love.

Changed

Wrap Up Exercises

1. What has God shown you as you worked through this 90 day devotional?

_____
_____
_____
_____
_____
_____
_____
_____

2. How have your thoughts, actions, and beliefs changed since Day 1?

_____
_____
_____
_____
_____
_____
_____
_____

3. Do you see God and your relationship with Him differently? If so explain How.

_____
_____
_____
_____
_____
_____
_____
_____

4. Explain what you'll do so you can hear, "Well done My good and faithful servant." on the day you meet Jesus.

_____
_____
_____
_____
_____
_____
_____
_____

Pastor Glenn

ABOUT THE AUTHOR

Glenn Hamel is a husband, father, pastor, author, and director. He is the recipient of Wakulla's "Distinguished Leadership" and "Heart of Wakulla" awards, Life Recovery Coach, Graduate of Liberty University, trained in addictions recovery. In addition, he has over 20 years of experience as director of Promise Land's faith-based recovery centers. Pastor Glenn can motivate and encourage readers uniquely and practically. Being passionate about God and his family, Glenn has had the privilege of serving in the ministry with his wife, Vera, since the day they married. They have devoted their lives to serving the rejected, hurting, abused, and addicted. They believe that loving and helping others is the best way to honor God. Together, they have raised seven children and numerous foster children.

www.GlennHamel.com

Also by Glenn Hamel

Pastor Glenn Hamel's books are down-to-earth and practical. His writings break down complicated spiritual teachings in an easily understandable way. Created - Defined by God will help you find God's plan for you and who He created you to be. Promise Land - Exile to Redemption will take on Pastor Glenn's journey into ministry and the development of the Promise Land Ministries Recovery Centers.

Promise Land - Exile to Redemption
Take a walk through Pastor Glenn's call to the ministry. See how God painfully demolished and then Divinely rebuilt Pastor Glenn and Promise Land. Read the stories, hear the miracles, and know that God has a plan for you.

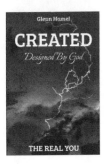

Created - Designed By God
When you know who you are, you know what to do! Ever wondered why you do what you do? Do you want to know why you keep falling for the enemy's tricks? Have you ever asked: "Why am I here, what is my purpose," or "What does God want me to do?" "Created" will take you on a journey to answer all of those questions and more. So if you're ready to defeat the enemy, overcome your struggles, find the real you, and live the life God designed for you, then "Created" is the book for you.

Pastor Glenn

Made in the USA
Columbia, SC
25 May 2024